Jesus

Who he is and why he matters

Alister McGrath

Inter-Varsity Press

INTER-VARSITY PRESS
38 De Montfort Street, Leicester LE1 7GP, UK

© Alister McGrath, 1987, 1994

Unless otherwise stated, Scripture quotations in this
publication are from the Holy Bible, New International
Version. Copyright © 1973, 1978, 1984 International Bible
Society. Published in Great Britain by Hodder & Stoughton
Ltd.

First published in this revised edition 1994. Original edition
(1987) published as *Understanding Jesus: Who Jesus is and why
he matters*.

Reprinted 1996

British Library Cataloguing in Publication Data
A catalogue record for this book is available from the British
Library.

ISBN 0-85110-878-4

Typeset in 9½ on 11½ point Palatino by Alister McGrath

Printed and bound in Great Britain by
Cox & Wyman Ltd, Reading, Berkshire.

*Inter-Varsity Press is the book-publishing division of the
Universities and Colleges Christian Fellowship (formerly the Inter-
Varsity Fellowship), a student movement linking Christian Unions
in universities and colleges throughout the United Kingdom and the
Republic of Ireland, and a member movement of the International
Fellowship of Evangelical Students. For information about local and
national activities write to UCCF, 38 De Montfort Street, Leicester
LE1 7GP.*

Contents

Introduction

Christianity continues to expand throughout the world. There is growing evidence of a new mood of confidence within the churches. Yet that mood does not ultimately rest upon anything to do with the churches themselves; rather, it reflects a new realization of the relevance and attractiveness of the person of Jesus Christ for the modern world.

Until very recently, there was a widespread belief in the western world that religious faith was fading away. Christians had been told that their faith was a thing of the past, something that the modern world could do without. The future had no place for Jesus Christ. Nobody is saying that any more. It is becoming more and more obvious that there is a renewed interest in religion in general, and Christianity in particular, in the West and far beyond. More and more people, of all ages and cultures, are encountering the remarkable and deeply fascinating figure of Jesus Christ. The collapse of many rival belief systems, especially Marxism, has led to a new interest in both Christianity and the person of Jesus.

This book aims to help those who wish to discover for themselves the identity and significance of Jesus Christ. It is not written from any denominational or party perspective, but aims to explain, as fully yet as simply as possible, the significance of Jesus Christ for the world. It assumes no prior knowledge of the Christian faith or Christian theology on the part of its readers.

In recent years, a major new trend has begun to develop in western culture. The radical period of reaction against anything that seemed to be 'traditional' is over. Many who rejected Christianity in the 1960s and 1970s are beginning to regret having done so. At the time, the new alternative ideas seemed exciting and dynamic. Christianity appeared to be old-fashioned and boring. But those new ideas and values have turned out to be like the emperor's new clothes – and so, often after many years, an older generation is beginning to regain an interest in Christianity. They are beginning to drift back to faith. Having studiously ignored or rejected Jesus Christ in their younger years, they are beginning to discover in him the 'bread of life' who is able to satisfy their deepest needs.

This book aims to explain the identity of Jesus to such people, and to allow them to gain an appreciation of this remarkable person. It will be of especial interest to those thinking about Christianity for the first time. However, it will also provide important and helpful material for those who have already discovered the wonder of the Christian faith, and want to deepen their understanding and appreciation of it, or who want to explain it to their friends.

1

Has Christianity got Jesus wrong?

Everyone loves a sensational story. The discovery of the long-lost tomb of the Egyptian pharaoh Tutankhamun in the 1920s was one of the greatest media events of the century. The spectacular exposure of the Watergate cover-up scandal half a century later by the *Washington Post* led to the dramatic resignation of Richard Nixon as President of the United States. Perhaps the greatest media scoop of all would be the total discrediting of a major world religion. For example, if it could be conclusively shown that Mohammed never existed, or that the Koran was a later fabrication, the credibility of Islam would collapse.

Yet it is Christianity which has borne the brunt of the continuing media search for sensationalism. In practice, the western media has shown little interest in attacking or attempting to discredit Islam, or any religion other than Christianity, apparently partly on account of the fear of being accused of hostility towards ethnic minorities. Christianity predominates in the West, so media attention has been focused almost entirely upon the documents and central figure of this faith – namely, the gospels and the person of Jesus Christ. People who don't like religion of any kind tend to focus their attention on Christianity, and especially Jesus himself.

Anti-Christian attitudes in the West

TV chat show hosts are always anxious to increase their audience ratings through any form of sensationalism, just as publishers are always enthusiastic about higher sales. So books that suggest that Christians have got Jesus totally wrong get a lot of attention. Nobody in the West at the moment cares much about books which argue that Islam is a human fabrication. Jesus is different. He matters. The ferocity and frequency of attacks on the historicity of Jesus Christ is a telling indication of how deeply his influence is felt throughout the western world, and how deeply threatened many people feel as a consequence. Many Christians are discouraged and saddened by such attacks, especially by the high media profile given to the critics of Christianity, and the failure to give equal space to Christian rebuttals of such sensationalist stories. Sadly, there is little that can be done about this. In an age dominated by a concern to achieve high sales and audience ratings, sensationalist stories will invariably take priority over the patient and considered work of serious scholarship.

Of all the world's religions, it is Christianity which has had to bear the brunt of anti-religious assaults since the late seventeenth century. Christianity is widely regarded as the 'Establishment religion' in the West. As a result, more radical writers tend to see the discrediting of Christianity as an important aspect of their anti-Establishment programme. In different cultural contexts these writers could well be among Christianity's most vigorous supporters, as can be seen from their attitudes to

Lutheranism in the former East Germany, to Roman Catholicism in Poland under the period of Soviet domination, and to the Coptic Christians in Egypt under assault from Moslem fundamentalists. But in the West, there is much credibility to be gained in elitist circles through challenging the credibility of Christianity. Interestingly, to challenge Judaism or Islam in this way would be seen to amount to the persecution or harassment of a minority group. The charge of anti-Semitism could easily be brought against someone criticizing aspects of Judaism. Anyone in the West who attacked Islam would probably be criticized for failing to respect the rights of a minority. They might even be accused of being racist. Christianity, being a majority presence, has had to bear the brunt of a broadly anti-religious agenda in the West. And all too often, this centres on a full frontal attack on the historicity and character of Jesus Christ.

The situation is made worse by the anti-religious agenda which is gaining the upper hand in western universities. Many academics are openly sceptical and scathing about Christianity. To understand why, we need to go back to the 1960s, when it seemed as if a new age was about to dawn. In the United States, the civil rights movement blossomed, there were mass protests against the Vietnam war, and tens of thousands packed into the tiny town of Woodstock to hear the music of the coming generation. In Paris, students rioted, protesting against the Establishment. Something new and irresistible seemed to be about to happen. And it was generally agreed that the future held no place for religion. John Lennon asked us to imagine a 'world without religion', a sort of agnostic paradise on earth.

In the end, it all came to nothing. It was a dream, and nothing more. Religion has made a powerful comeback, and is widely recognized as one of the most potent factors in modern international politics. But there were many who grew up in the 1960s who cherished the vision of a world without religion. And many of them are today in senior positions in colleges, high schools and universities. The result? High school and college students are often put under the authority of men and women who have a deep-rooted hostility towards any religion. One recent survey suggested that 30% of American college professors had no religious commitment of any kind. An anti-Christian bias is developing, with intense hostility being channelled towards Jesus Christ. The simplest form of expressing this hostility is to deny his existence or relevance, or to assert that he has been totally misunderstood or deliberately misrepresented by Christians, and dismiss anyone who disagrees with this as a crank or a fundamentalist. This is very distressing for Christian students, who often find themselves coming under pressure to conform to the views of their teachers, or who are made to feel isolated and foolish by the scathing hostility they experience towards their faith.

Rationalist criticisms of Jesus Christ

The intellectual basis of these trends can be traced back to the late eighteenth century, with the dawn of the period of history usually known as the Enlightenment. The period of rationalism in Europe, usually regarded as having begun in the eighteenth century, showed little taste for ideas such as Jesus being a divine saviour. It was argued that such ideas were actually due to early Christians misunderstanding or misrepresenting the New Testament, and that it was possible to rediscover the *real* Jesus by approaching the New Testament in a different way. If Jesus was anything, according to the rationalists, he was a good moral teacher.

One eighteenth century writer (Hermann Samuel Reimarus) argued that the resurrection was little more than a 'cover-up', designed to get around the embarrassing and unexpected premature death of Jesus. It was, he argued, pure invention, cooked up by the disciples, who couldn't cope with the harsh reality of the shameful death of Jesus. As a result, he suggested that the idea of the 'resurrection' ought to be eliminated from the New Testament, as a crude Christian invention. Much the same points re-emerge in discussion of the question today. Every now and then, however, the debate gets more interesting, as languishing writers of fiction or radical bishops join in the fun, adding a slight dash of literary sophistication or whiff of ecclesiastical scandal to an otherwise rather stale debate.

So the 'Quest for the Historical Jesus' (as the movement came to be known) got under way. Where first century writers had got Jesus wrong, it was argued, nineteenth or twentieth century writers could get him right. Perhaps this suggestion should have been viewed with considerably more scepticism than it actually encountered. But the fact remains that some nineteenth century New Testament scholars felt that it was possible to recover the 'real' Jesus from the Jesus of Christianity.

It should be appreciated that these scholars were generally writing at the peak of a movement which fervently believed that it was possible to write history 'as it actually was'. Many historians then thought that they could reconstruct the past exactly as it happened. By the middle of the twentieth century, this approach was widely regarded as hopelessly optimistic and naive. However, It exercized a deep influence over many earlier writers, who genuinely expected to be able to deliver a finely-detailed portrait of Jesus Christ, which differed radically from that offered by Christianity.

Jesus was just a moral teacher

According to these scholars, the early church got Jesus completely wrong. He wasn't God incarnate or a divine saviour, but a simple moral teacher, whose views on most things happened (remarkably!) to coincide with those of his nineteenth century rediscoverers. Jesus was the teacher of the 'fatherhood of God and the brotherhood of man'. It was an essentially simple and modern message, for which the first eighteen centuries of the Christian church were totally unprepared, and were obliged to leave to modern scholars to take up. The pearl of great price, having only just been dug up, was immediately reburied, in the hope that some wise and benevolent professor of theology might rediscover it centuries later.

Yet a healthy degree of scepticism is in order here. Is it likely that people living nineteen hundred years after the death of Jesus, and sharing nothing of his culture, his background, his language and his presuppositions, should be able to get Jesus right, when his contemporaries, who shared that culture, background, language and those presuppositions should have got him so terribly wrong? And the fact that the rediscovered Jesus was practically the mirror image of his rediscoverers was purely fortuitous! It just so happened that Jesus actually taught all the right things by the standards of the nineteenth century (the principles which ensure the healthy progress of civilisation, morality, and so on). Surely someone would have noticed that something was wrong here?

The possibility that these idealist theologians of the nineteenth century might just have projected their own moral ideas and aspirations onto a distant historical figure about whom they knew practically nothing, in order to discredit a different understanding of the identity and significance of Jesus for which they cared even less, never seems to have entered their heads. Since then we have been presented with lots of rediscovered figures of Jesus. He was a freedom fighter, an itinerant Kantian, a hypnotist, a mushroom-eater, a confused prophet, and an enthusiastic advocate of political correctness, to name but a few.

It is difficult to avoid the impression that there are a lot of people arguing that, whatever Jesus was, he *definitely wasn't* the divine saviour of sinful human beings that Christians have always thought he was. Because Jesus couldn't, as a matter of principle, be God incarnate, they argued, he must have been something else. Curiously, their views on what Jesus really was turned out to be even more unbelievable, although it took some time for this point to be fully appreciated. We shall explore one of the main problems in what follows.

The gospels and history

A consideration of the nature of the gospels will allow these reconstructions of Jesus to be seen in a corrective light. The gospels are written from the standpoint of faith, with the aim of bringing their readers to the point where they can share that faith. This means that the gospels are far more than biographies of Jesus, even though they include a substantial amount of biographical material. They aim to explain who Jesus is, and why he matters so much to the human race.

We may begin exploring this point by reflecting on

some immortal words from Edmund Clerihew Bentley's *Biography for Beginners*:

> The art of Biography
> Is different from Geography.
> Geography is about maps,
> But Biography is about chaps.

While we may be able to distinguish between geography and biography without too much difficulty, it is considerably more difficult to distinguish between biography and theology in the gospels. The gospel writers were not biographers, or even historians, by our standards, nor were they interested in providing an account of absolutely everything that Jesus said and did. For example, occasionally it does not seem to have mattered to them exactly at what point in his ministry Jesus told a particular parable. The important thing was that he *did* tell it, and that it was realized to be relevant to the preaching of the early church.

It is clear that the gospels of Matthew, Mark and Luke draw upon common material, although at times we encounter material which is peculiar to one, or two gospels. The term 'Synoptic Gospels' is often used to refer to these three gospels, as they can be set out in parallel columns to provide a summary (Greek: *synopsis*) of the life, death and resurrection of Jesus. The same material is sometimes presented in one setting in Mark, another in Matthew, and perhaps even a third in Luke. The same story may be told from different perspectives in different gospels. Sometimes a story is told at greater length in one gospel than in another. It is, however, evident that there is a solid historical core underlying the slight variations encountered in the gospel accounts.

New Testament scholarship has merely clarified the nature of this historical core, rather than called it into question. Again, it is necessary to emphasize that sensationalist writings which challenge this point are often given very high media profiles, whereas those which confirm their reliability are generally passed over in silence. The gospel writers were concerned to remain utterly faithful to the accounts of the life, death and resurrection of Jesus which had been handed down to them. There can be no doubt whatsoever that the gospel accounts of Jesus contain a solid base of historical information, linked with an interpretation of this information. Biography and theology are interwoven to such an extent that they cannot be separated any more.

The early Christians were convinced that Jesus was the Messiah, the Son of God, and their Saviour, and naturally felt that these conclusions should be passed on to their readers, along with any biographical details which helped cast light on them. It is for this reason that fact and interpretation are so thoroughly intermingled in the gospels. The first Christians had no doubt that their theological interpretation of Jesus was right, and that it was therefore an important fact which should be included in their 'biographies'.

With this point in mind, let us return to the ill-fated 'Quest for the Historical Jesus'. The basic assumption which lay behind this movement was that the gospels did nothing more than set out some facts about the history of Jesus. It was then up to the readers of the gospels to interpret these facts in any way they liked. Or, to put it another way, the gospels were treated as raw data which required interpretation. We now know that this is quite unacceptable. The gospels are not purely factual accounts of the life and teaching of Jesus; they blend together history and theology, event and interpretation.

The gospels are thus not raw data which require interpretation, but are instead interpretations of raw data. Furthermore, the process of selection which is such an important feature of the 'period of oral transmission' means that much information concerning Jesus (which the early Christians thought insignificant for their purposes) is forever lost. At first sight, this might seem to be a worrying possibility. Surely all information about Jesus is of vital importance?

Yet on further reflection, it can be seen that this is not the case. We do not know the colour of Jesus' hair. We do not know his height, his blood group or his shoe size. Why not? Because the first Christians regarded such things as trivial and irrelevant, in the light of the much more significant conclusion that Jesus Christ brought forgiveness, life and hope to a dark and lost world. Everything else is overshadowed by this. The colour of Jesus' hair or the size of his feet is totally eclipsed by the joyful news that the world is offered eternal life through his death and resurrection.

As a result, sceptical readers of the gospels do not have access to the material which they need if they are to attempt a realistic 'reinterpretation' of Jesus. Instead, they are forced to rely on speculation and unproved hypotheses rather than rigorous historical analysis. The gospels are written from the standpoint of faith in the crucified and risen Jesus, and reflect the faith of the early Christians to such an extent that it is actually impossible to distinguish between 'event' and 'interpretation' at point after point of vital importance. The gospels are written in the light of the fundamental conviction that Jesus is 'the Christ, the Son of the living God' (Matthew

16:16), and their content cannot be isolated from this conviction.

This point presents no problems whatsoever for the Christian reader of the gospel, who shares the faith of the gospel writers concerning the identity and significance of Jesus Christ. It does, however, raise certain fundamental difficulties for those who do not share this faith. Basically, the gospels are out to win their readers over to their point of view about the identity and significance of Jesus, by setting those readers alongside the disciples as they come to faith, in order that they may share the same experience. But readers who are convinced that the first Christians were wrong in their understanding of the identity and significance of Jesus (and hence that the gospels are wrong at certain crucial points) are faced with three possible options.

(1). They may argue that the gospels allow them to develop a different interpretation of the identity and significance of Jesus, which they find more acceptable. This is basically the approach of the 'Quest for the Historical Jesus' movement. This approach is initially attractive, but on further reflection is obviously impossible. To reinterpret Jesus requires access to information which is no longer available to us – the *complete* history of Jesus Christ, absolutely everything which he said and did, as well as a total familiarity with the first century Palestinian culture in which his ministry took place. This history is for ever lost to us. Naturally, it is very exciting for sensationalist writers or journalists to suggest that some aspects of this 'lost history' were deliberately suppressed by Christians, because of their negative implications for faith. But as often as these elaborate conspiracy theories are raised, they fail to convince for lack of evidence.

19

All that we possess of the history of Jesus, apart from some scattered references in Roman historians, is what we find in the gospels, and it will be obvious that the gospel writers have been selective in regard to what they included. One of the reasons why theories about reading between the lines of the Dead Sea Scrolls are so attractive to some non-Christians, more anxious to discredit the Christian position than to understand it, is that these approaches are held to offer access to allegedly 'unbiased' information about Jesus, in contrast to the 'biased' accounts of the New Testament. In fact, these theories generally amount to little more than fantasy, involving the construction of imaginary historical worlds on the basis of flimsy and intensely disputed pieces of historical evidence. Yet their inventors wanted to believe in them. They preferred their own ideas about what Jesus was like. Furthermore, history and theology, event and interpretation, are intermingled to such an extent that they cannot be separated with the accuracy and precision which such a radical reinterpretation would require.

The 'reinterpretation' of Jesus on the basis of the New Testament accounts is thus a blind alley, which leads nowhere. It is, of course, possible to base a 'reinterpretation' of Jesus on something other than the gospels, such as preconceived ideas about God or human nature. It will be clear that this is of little relevance to the Christian understanding of the identity and significance of Christ, particularly as Christians have generally based their understandings of God and human nature upon Jesus, rather than the other way round. In view of the importance of this point, we may explore it a little further.

The argument really concerns how we know anything about God in the first place. The Christian argues that the person of Jesus is the most reliable source of knowledge about God to be had, whereas others may argue you can learn about him from the star-studded night sky, stunning sunsets, inspired performances of Mozart flute concertos or beautiful paintings. We shall return to this argument later. However, at this point we can stress that human reason is at best capable of giving very limited insights into the nature and purposes of God. It can point us in the right direction, but there is still a very long way to go.

A specific example may make this point clearer. Someone might suggest that, as God is absolutely beyond this world, he could not have become incarnate in Jesus Christ. So the idea that Jesus is God must be rejected as ridiculous from the outset. But where does this suggestion come from? How does anyone know that God cannot become incarnate? How can anyone be sure that this is what God is really like? Has anyone access to some source of knowledge denied to everyone else, which allows them to make such certain statements about exactly what God can and cannot do? They conclude that God cannot have become incarnate in Jesus Christ. Jesus Christ cannot be God incarnate.

Yet somehow, the conclusion of this argument appears to have been presupposed! Far from being the end product of a long and reasoned discussion, the conclusion was predetermined at its beginning, by someone who has already decided that God cannot become incarnate. By definition, not only cannot Jesus be God incarnate; nobody can! And just what is the evidence for this? Someone's dogmatic assertion, based on their private view of what God can and cannot do, owing nothing to the Christian view of God, and everything to their own imagination. Theology cannot and need not put up with such dogmatism! One of the greatest paradoxes is that those who criticize the 'dogmatism' of traditional views of the identity of Jesus often turn out to be equally dogmatic about their own more radical views!

The Christian, however, argues the other way round: because God did become incarnate in Jesus Christ, we must learn to reject any concept of God as totally beyond this world, and uninvolved in it. Preconceived ideas about God must be abandoned, to be replaced with the God who we see, know and meet in Jesus Christ. Jesus Christ provides us with the most complete and reliable picture of God we can have this side of our resurrection.

(2). Such critics may reject the gospels completely, and have nothing to do with them. This is an intellectually honest approach, but one which is not likely to commend itself to Christological sceptics!

(3). These critics may approach the gospels in the spirit in which they were written, either sharing the faith of the gospel writers, or allowing themselves to be carried along with them. Once more, this approach has the virtue of intellectual honesty. They may wish to attempt to restate the convictions of the gospel writers in terms more comprehensible to the modern reader, but they are still operating within the framework of faith established by the gospels.

The new understanding of the nature of the gospels which has developed over the last century cannot be said to have eroded confidence in the reliability of the New Testament portrayal of Christ, despite the swashbuckling claims of over-enthusiastic critics of Christianity. New Testament scholarship has established that the gospels are a remarkable, probably a unique form of writing, and has helped us to understand the purposes, intentions and priorities of their writers with greater confidence. As we shall see, however, this approach devastates a number of rival approaches to the identity and significance of Jesus.

The demolition of liberal approaches to Jesus

One key figure linked with the modern critical approach to the New Testament was the great German New Testament scholar Rudolf Bultmann (1884–1976). In the course of his writings, Bultmann emphasised two points in particular. First, the critical approach to the New Testament cut the ground from under liberal Christologies (such as Jesus as just a 'moral teacher' or 'religious hero' or 'moral example'). Secondly, there was an urgent need to restate the content of the New Testament portrayal of Christ in terms that modern humanity could understand.

For Bultmann, the New Testament understands Jesus as an act of God, totally distinct from anything else. This understanding of the identity and significance of Jesus is deeply embedded in the New Testament, particularly the gospels, to the extent that it was quite impossible to find any other picture of Jesus portrayed in its pages. Bultmann thus singled out three understandings of the identity and significance of Jesus which could no longer be taken seriously.

1. That Jesus was just a good religious teacher, like Moses.

2. That Jesus was a religious hero, who died to make some sort of religious point.

3. That Jesus' significance lay in his religious personality or his consciousness of the presence of God.

According to Bultmann, the foundations of all these were shattered beyond repair by the rise of the critical study of the New Testament. The only understanding of the identity and significance of Jesus which could stand up in the light of New Testament scholarship was that of a unique divine act in human history. How Bultmann went on to explain this divine act does not concern us here, and is actually not relevant to our discussion. What is important is the realization that if any understanding of the identity and significance of Jesus has been irredeemably discredited by modern New Testament scholarship, it is not the 'traditional' picture of Christ as divine, but the views of the 'rediscoverers of the historical Jesus' and their modern-day followers.

Of course, there are still those who wish to suggest that Jesus was a misunderstood religious genius, or hero, or just a lunatic. There will almost certainly always be views like this in circulation. But what needs to be emphasized is that they cannot be supported by responsible use of the New Testament documents, and particularly the gospels, as sources. As we are almost totally dependent upon precisely these sources for our knowledge of Jesus, this virtually amounts to the elimination of such totally inadequate portrayals of the identity and significance of Jesus Christ. It is ironical, to say the least, that some critics of traditional Christianity appeal to Bultmann in support of their views about Jesus being a moral example, or a religious teacher, apparently quite unaware that it was against exactly these views that Bultmann directed his devastating criticisms!

The gospels: committed and so biased?
What of the suggestion that the New Testament documents, especially the gospels, are biased sources, and thus cannot be trusted? This point is often raised in discussion of this subject, both at street level and in more academic contexts. It is pointed out, with reason, that the

gospel writers were committed to Jesus. As a result, they are prejudiced, and incapable of providing an objective picture of Jesus. How important is this criticism?

The potential bias of any historical source is of major importance, and cannot be ignored. A Christian source of the period is likely to show pro-Christian bias, just as a Jewish source might well be expected to be anti-Christian. Identification of possible bias is important in assessing possible variations in weight to be given to different sources.

Yet it must be stressed that a source can be committed and correct at one and the same time. An example will make this clear. During the Second World War, the German Nazi leader, Adolf Hitler, initiated an extermination programme directed against Jews and others in areas of Europe occupied by the Nazis. A programme of mass murder was undertaken. Gradually, news of this campaign of genocide (often referred to as 'the Holocaust') filtered through to the outside world, especially the United States of America.

However, the initial reports of what was going on at the Nazi extermination camps came from Jews, who were regarded as having vested interests in the matter. Their reports were often dismissed as 'biased'. As a result, the recognition of the horrifying facts of the Holocaust was delayed in the United States. It was not appreciated that committed witnesses, caught up in and involved in the events in question, could nevertheless be reliable witnesses. A witness to a particularly horrifying or thrilling event is bound to be affected by what he or she has seen. Yet that does not diminish the potential reliability of his or her witness to what has happened.

Precisely the same point needs to be made in relation to the New Testament writings. They are indeed written from the standpoint of faith, and with the object of bringing their readers to faith. But it does not follow that they are unreliable. The writings themselves stress their evidential and historical foundations. For Paul, the resurrection was a public event, open to challenge and verification by the five hundred or so who had witnessed it (1 Corinthians 15:3–8). The gospel is not about 'cleverly-invented stories', but rests upon eyewitness accounts of the 'power and coming of our Lord Jesus Christ' (2 Peter 1:16). John stresses that he and others have witnessed the grounds of the Christian faith, and are concerned to pass on to others this deep sense of assurance and confidence (1 John 1:1–4). Some will continue to argue that the gospels cannot be taken seriously because they are written by committed individuals from the standpoint of faith. But that commitment might just be the result of the reliability of the foundations of this gospel, and the enormous attraction of the person of Jesus Christ!

In the first part of this work, we shall begin to discover something of this remarkable person, and understand why he has had such a deep impact on so many people. We begin by considering the relation between Jesus and the Christian faith.

Part 1

Getting started

2

Jesus and Christianity

At the heart of the Christian faith lies, not so much a set of abstract ideas or beliefs, but a person – one of the most attractive and intriguing figures that the world has ever known. It is this person who stands at the centre of the Christian gospel, and who gives the Christian faith its distinctive shape and form. It cannot be said too often that the gospel is not about abstract ideas, but about a living person. Christianity is not some form of 'ism', like Marxism, Darwinism or Hegelianism. These are all abstract systems of thought which have become detached from the person of their founder, and reduced simply to sets of doctrines. (Have you noticed how quickly these seem to go out of date? It's as if 'isms' quickly become 'wasms'!)

Although the ideas which we call 'Marxism' were originally developed by the nineteenth-century German political philosopher Karl Marx, the ideas are now quite independent of him. All that Marx did was to introduce them. The relationship between Jesus and Christianity is, however, quite different. At the heart of the Christian faith is the person of Jesus Christ. Christianity is not just

29

the teachings of Jesus Christ. It *is* Jesus Christ, in all his potential to transform our situation and lives.

Christians have always insisted that there was something special, something qualitatively different about Jesus, which sets him apart from religious teachers or thinkers, and demands careful consideration. There is a close connection between the person and the message of Jesus. It is the person of Jesus – who he was, what he did, and the impact which he made on those who encountered him – which make his message important. From the outset, Christians appear to have realized that Jesus just could not be treated as an ordinary human being. There is no way in which Christians view Jesus simply as one more religious teacher or prophet in the course of the long history of the human race. Jesus is different. Yet in what ways is he different? And what do these differences rest on?

Let us begin by noticing that there is a close connection between the person and the message of Jesus. It is the person of Jesus – who he was, what he did, and the impact which he made on those who encountered him – which make his message important. From the outset, Christians appear to have realized that Jesus just could not be treated as an ordinary human being. There was something different about him. But what?

The main answer to this question is as electrifying as it is difficult. Jesus is to be recognized as the living God, who has entered into our history to meet us and bring us home to him. From the earliest times Christians worshipped and adored Jesus as if he were God. While recognizing the difficulties – and even the dangers – of speaking in this way, Christians insisted that, in a very real sense, Jesus is the whole of the gospel message. When Christians talk about God, they actually mean God

30

as he has been revealed to us in the person of Jesus Christ. This is no artificial dogma; rather, it is the only way of making sense of the evidence we find in the New Testament concerning Jesus Christ, including his cruxifixion and resurrection.

Who do you say that I am?

The gospels tell us that as Jesus was walking with his disciples in the region of Caesarea Philippi, he suddenly asked them a question: 'Who do people say I am?' The disciples replied with a variety of answers – they told him that some people thought that he was John the Baptist, others Elijah, or some other prophet. Jesus then asked his disciples the crucial question, which demanded that they speak for themselves, instead of merely reporting the opinions of others. 'But what about you? Who do *you* say I am?' And Peter replied for them all when he answered: 'You are the Christ' (Mark 8:27–29).The central challenge posed to the reader of the New Testament, especially the four gospels, concerns the identity and relevance of Jesus Christ.

In Jesus, the message and the messenger are one and the same. Jesus' message is given weight and status because of who we recognize Jesus to be. As we shall see later, the resurrection of Jesus appears to have been the decisive factor in forcing the first Christians to begin to take the astonishing – but to them necessary and appropriate – step of thinking of Jesus as God, in some sense of the word. We could put this more formally by saying that Jesus Christ is the object of faith, rather than just an example of faith. The challenge posed to every succeeding generation by the New Testament witness to Jesus is not so much, 'What did he teach?', but 'Who is he? And what is his relevance for us?' Christianity does not claim to possess all truth. Yet if it loses sight of its central conviction that in Christ it has found access to the deepest truths about God and ourselves, it has lost itself.

'Who do *you* say that I am?' As we read the gospels, it is impossible to avoid the impression that we have met a real person. There are many historical characters who we may know much about from history books, such as Alexander the Great, Julius Caesar, George Washington or Admiral Nelson. Yet these historical figures fail to make a personal impression upon us. They remain figures from the past. There is a definite 'long, long ago and far, far away' kind of quality to our thinking about them. We do not feel we know them by personal acquaintance. We always seem to know them at second hand, only through the pages of history books. On the other hand, there are many fictional characters who never existed in reality, and yet whom we feel we 'know' as real people, such as Shakespeare's Falstaff, Mr Pickwick, or Sherlock Holmes.

There are remarkably few real historical characters who come across to us as personalities – people who we feel we can know personally. An obvious example would be Dr Samuel Johnson, as recorded for us by Boswell, who comes across as a rather grave and melancholy figure who still has a love of fun and nonsense ('The Irish are a fair people – they never speak well of one another'). Another is Socrates, as we find him in Plato's dialogues. But the most important of all is the Jesus we encounter in the gospels. Although he is a genuine historical figure who lived and died in an obscure and uninteresting part of the world two thousand years ago, he nevertheless comes across as someone we feel we know in the same sense as we know a real and living person – someone whom we can *know*, rather than just *know about.* As one of his more reluctant and sceptical admirers once wrote: 'We know no-one as well as we know Jesus'.

For precisely this reason, the figure of Jesus Christ continues to exercise a remarkable influence over many people who would not dream of regarding themselves as Christians. Many who would never think of coming to church find themselves being deeply attracted to Jesus Christ. There seems to be something about him which draws us to him. He is a deeply attractive figure, who intrigues, puzzles and delights those who read of him. It is almost as if people instinctively realize that Jesus is different from all others.

But what is it about Jesus that causes him to exercise such a remarkable and pervasive influence over men and women some two thousand years after his birth? What is it about him that gives rise to such interest? And how can we make sense of his identity and significance? It is with the unfolding and answering of these questions that this book is concerned.

Jesus really existed!

We may begin to explore the identity of Jesus by providing some basic historical information. Jesus was a first-century Jew, who lived in the area now known as Palestine in the reign of Tiberius Caesar, and who was executed by crucifixion under Pontius Pilate. The Roman historian Tacitus refers to Christians deriving their name from 'Christ, who was executed at the hands of the procurator Pontius Pilate in the reign of Tiberius' (*Annals*, xv, 44, 3). The historical evidence for his existence is sufficient to satisfy all but those who are determined to believe that he did not exist, whatever the evidence may be.

If the existence of Jesus is denied, despite all the evidence we possess which points to the opposite conclusion, consistency would demand that we should also deny the existence of an alarming number of historical figures, the evidence for whose existence is considerably more slender than that for Jesus. All the historical evidence we possess about the origins of Christianity points to a real historical figure lying behind it. Indeed, if Jesus did not exist as an historical figure, it would probably be necessary to suppose that someone remarkably like him did, in order to explain the evidence in our possession. Thus Paul takes Jesus' existence as a fact which does not require demonstration, and concentrates upon establishing and defending the significance of his life, death and resurrection.

Yet there are hidden motivations which lead some to want to question the historical existence of Jesus. Many belief-systems are deeply challenged and threatened by Christianity, and make it a point of principle to deny the existence of Jesus. An excellent example of this used to be provided by Marxism. During the period in which Marxism reigned in the Soviet Union, university students were told that Jesus Christ was simply a myth. Those unfortunate students had access to no alternative sources of knowledge. They had no way of challenging this pseudo-historical dogmatism on the part of their teachers. Even today, such unsubstantiated assertions are repeated in many western universities, often by anti-religious academics exploiting their privileged status in relation to their students. In fact, as we noted earlier, one of the greatest paradoxes of recent years is that an anti-Christian dogmatism even worse than that found in the old Soviet Union seems to be gaining ground in some American colleges and universities!

That Jesus did not exist is a dogmatic presupposition quite unacceptable to the unbiased historian, rather than an obvious – or even a plausible – conclusion of a detailed study of the evidence. Although there have been, and almost certainly always will be, those who argue that Jesus did not exist, who will doubtless continue to provide straws to be grasped by those determined to reject Christianity, the fact remains that they are simply not taken seriously by disinterested and impartial historical scholarship.

Jesus was crucified

So far, so good. What about the central Christian claim that Jesus was crucified under the Roman procurator Pontius Pilate? The theme of the cross of Jesus Christ is deeply embedded in the New Testament. One of the earliest literary witnesses to the central importance of the crucifixion is Paul's first letter to the Christian church at Corinth, which probably dates from the early months of 54 AD. In the first chapter of this letter, Paul lays considerable emphasis upon the fact that Christ was crucified. The subject of his preaching was 'Christ crucified' (1:23); the power lying behind the gospel proclamation is 'the cross of Christ' (1:17); the entire gospel can even be summarized as 'the message of the cross' (1:18). Jesus 'endured the cross, despising its shame' (Hebrews 12:2). The tradition of the crucifixion of Jesus Christ is deeply embedded in the New Testament witness to him at every level. It is impossible to account for this consistent emphasis, unless it is based upon an historical fact which was widely known and accepted at the time.

If the tradition concerning the crucifixion of Jesus was an invention of the first Christians, we can only conclude that it demonstrates that they were too stupid for words. The idea of a crucified saviour was immediately seized upon by the opponents of the early church as an absurdity, demonstrating the ridiculous nature of Christian claims. Justin Martyr, attempting to defend Christianity against its more sophisticated critics in the second century, conceded that the Christian proclamation of a crucified Christ appeared to be madness: '[The opponents of Christianity] say that our madness lies in the fact that we put a crucified man in second place to the unchangeable and eternal God, the creator of the world.'

For a Jew, anyone hanged upon a tree was to be regarded as cursed by God (Deuteronomy 21:23), which would hardly commend the Christian claim that Jesus was indeed the long-awaited Messiah. Indeed, one of the Dead Sea scrolls suggests that crucifixion was regarded as the proper form of execution for a Jew suspected of high treason. Yet the first Christians regarded the preaching of the gospel to Jews as one of their top priorities. Why would they include an idea which would have been so deeply offensive to a Jewish audience? The answer is quite simple: they had to. It was an historical fact, known to all, which had to be acknowledged and preached, even if it could lead to the alienation of many potential Jewish converts.

It is clear from contemporary evidence that crucifixion was a widespread form of execution within the Roman Empire, and that there was an astonishing variety of manners in which this execution might be carried out. It is impossible to define what form a 'normal' crucifixion might take: the victim was generally flogged or tortured beforehand, and then might be tied or nailed to the cross in practically any position, subject only to the ingenuity and perversity of the executioner. Far from being an essentially bloodless form of execution, as some commentators have suggested, the victim would have bled profusely. Only if he had not been flogged or tortured previously, and bound, rather than nailed to the cross, would no blood have been spilled.

This form of punishment appears to have been employed ruthlessly to suppress rebellions in the Roman provinces, such as the revolt of the Cantabrians in northern Spain, as well as those of the Jews. Josephus' accounts of the crucifixion of countless Jewish fugitives who attempted to escape from besieged Jerusalem at the time of its final destruction by Roman armies make horrifying reading. In the view of most Roman jurists, notorious criminals should be crucified on the exact location of their crime, so that 'the sight may deter others from such crimes'. Perhaps for this reason, the Roman emperor Quintillian crucified criminals on the busiest thoroughfares, in order that the maximum deterrent effect might be achieved.

It is therefore little wonder that the sophisticated pagan world of the first century reacted with disbelief and disgust to the Christians' suggestion that they should take seriously 'an evil man and his cross' (*homo noxius et crux eius*) to the point of worshipping him. Crucifixion was a punishment reserved for the lowest criminals, clearly implying that Jesus belonged to this category of people.

If the early Christians had based their message upon a fictitious figure, or upon a real figure who they deliberately misrepresented, they would have been fools to portray Jesus as having been *crucified*. Nothing could have been calculated to have evoked a more universal negative reaction on the part of their audience as the early Christians proclaimed the gospel. Were the first

Christians *really* that stupid? Would they have invented such a story, which could only be used against them? Once more, there is no reason for any except a dogmatic critic, who is determined to disbelieve each and every statement made by the New Testament concerning Jesus as a matter of principle, to call into question the historical nature of the crucifixion of Jesus.

Events and their meanings

But it is at this point that we must pause to reflect. The Christian faith certainly presupposes that Jesus existed as a real historical figure, and that he was crucified. Christianity is, however, most emphatically not about the mere facts that Jesus existed and was crucified. Let us recall some words of Paul:

> Now, brothers, I want to remind you of the gospel I preached to you, which you received and on which you have taken your stand. By this gospel you are saved . . . For what I received I passed on to you as of first importance: that Christ died for our sins according to the Scriptures, that he was buried, that he was raised on the third day according to the Scriptures, and that he appeared to Peter, and then to the Twelve [Apostles] (1 Corinthians 15:1–5).

The use of the words 'passed on' is very significant. They are drawn from the technical language of tradition, of 'handing down' or 'handing over', and point to the fact that Paul is passing on to his readers something that had earlier been passed on to him. In other words, Paul was not the first to summarize the Christian faith in terms of the two essential components of Christ's crucifixion and resurrection. He had learned this from others. Paul is not here relying on his own memory at this point, but on the collective memory of a much larger group of people.

It is widely believed that Paul is here reciting a formula, a form of words, which was in general use in the early church, and which he had received – not just in general terms, but in almost exactly the form which he passes down to the Corinthian Christians. He is not relying on his own memory, but on that of the Christian church in the earliest period of its existence. Earlier in this letter, Paul had made clear that the content of his preaching to the Corinthian Christians, upon which their faith was based, was 'Christ crucified' (1:17–18; 2:2). Two important points must be noted.

(1). Paul asserts that the Christ who was crucified and buried was 'raised on the third day'. For Paul, the death of Christ was followed by his resurrection from the dead. Paul's exposition of the significance of Jesus Christ for humanity is based upon his linking these two events. But whereas it was commonplace for people to be crucified at the time, we possess no account of any other crucified individual being raised from the dead. Indeed, there appears to have been no other case of resurrection in the course of human history. This has prompted some critics to suggest that the event never, in fact, took place. We shall consider this suggestion later. But it is notable that Paul links Jesus' death and resurrection together as the two central elements of his gospel. Jesus 'was delivered over to death for our sins, and was raised to life for our justification' (Romans 4:25).

(2). Paul makes a clear distinction between the *event* of the death of Christ, and the *significance* of this event. That Christ died is a simple matter of history; that Christ died *for our sins* is the gospel itself. Even if it could be demonstrated to the satisfaction of the most biased opponent of Christianity that Jesus Christ really did exist, and that he died upon a cross, this would not strictly amount to a proof of the truth of the Christian faith. The Christian faith is based upon certain historical events, but is not to be identified with those events alone: it is to be identified with a particular interpretation of these events.

The distinction between an *event* and its *meaning* must be appreciated. This can be illustrated from an event which took place in 49 BC, when the great Roman commander Julius Caesar crossed a small river with a legion of soldiers. That river was the Rubicon, and it marked an important frontier within the Roman Empire. It was the boundary between Italy and Cisalpine Gaul, a colonized region to the north-west of Italy in modern-day France. As an event, it was not especially important. The Rubicon was not a great river, and there was no particular difficulty in crossing it. People have crossed wider and deeper rivers before and since. As a simple event, it was not remarkable. But that is not why the crossing of that river was important. It is the meaning of the event that guarantees its place in the history books, for the political significance of that event was enormous. Crossing this national frontier with an army was a deliberate act of rebellion against Rome. It marked a declaration of war on the part of Caesar against Pompey and the Roman senate. The event was the crossing of a river; the meaning of that event was a declaration of war.

In many ways, the death of Christ may be said to parallel Caesar's crossing of the Rubicon. The event itself appears unexceptional, except to those who know its significance. The Rubicon was a small river, and it was not difficult to cross. People had crossed much wider rivers before and since then. As an event, it hardly seems significant. Similarly, Jesus died upon a cross. Everyone has to die sometime. On the basis of contemporary records, we know that an incalculable number of people died in this way at that time. Jesus would not have been alone in being executed in this way. As an event, the crucifixion hardly seems important or noteworthy.

On the other hand, those aware of the meaning of an event saw behind the mere external event itself, to what it signified, to the reason why it was important. Pompey and the Roman senate were not interested in the mechanics of how Caesar crossed the Rubicon: for them, it meant war. Similarly, Paul was not particularly interested in the mechanics of the crucifixion of Jesus; for him, it meant salvation, forgiveness and victory over death. Thus the 'message of the cross' was not concerned with the simple fact that Jesus was crucified, but with the significance of this event for us. Jesus died, in order that we might live. Jesus was numbered among sinners, so that sinners might be forgiven.

This leads to a very significant conclusion. It is possible to observe the event of the crucifixion, without being aware of the meaning of the cross. Two people may be in the same position, and yet see something quite different. Every now and then books with titles like *Great Moments from English Literature* make their appearance, aiming to familiarize their readers with some of the greatest passages from the rich pastures of English writings. I think we can safely say that the following lines by Frederick Langbridge (1849–1923) will not feature prominently in them!

> Two men look out through the same bars:
> One sees the mud, and one the stars.

Langbridge asks us to imagine two people in prison, looking out through the same window. Although they share the same vantage point, they nevertheless see very different things. The point that Langbridge makes is that some people see nothing but the rut of everyday life, ending in death, while others raise their eyes to heaven, knowing that their ultimate destiny lies with God. Their situation is identical; their outlooks are totally different. They see the same things, but from a very different perspective.

Much the same is true of the cross. Imagine two people, watching Jesus Christ die upon the cross on that first Good Friday, all those years ago. One might see nothing more than an everyday execution of an unimportant Jew. The other might see the Saviour of the world dying, in order that the world might be saved. One sees Jesus as a criminal dying for his own sins. The other sees him as the Son of God, dying for our sins. Each observer sees the same event; they place very different interpretations upon it. In fact, one of the turning points in many people's personal journey to faith is often the realization that they have been treating the cross simply as a distant historical event. Once they appreciate that the cross is about forgiveness, rather than just history, a door seems to open, leading to a new understanding of the relevance of the gospel to their lives. That Jesus died is history; that Jesus died *for us* is the gospel itself.

On the basis of this, it will be clear that Christianity is not just about the historical fact of the cross; it is about realizing its full meaning. That Jesus died is a statement about an historical event; that Jesus died for us is a statement about the meaning of that event, and is nothing less than the gospel itself.

The importance of perspective

We are not talking simply about different ways of looking at the same thing. All of us are used to the fact that a painting which seems to be grotesque to one onlooker appears to be nothing less than inspired to another. For example, in the 1980s, there was considerable excitement about an exhibit which made its way around leading art galleries in New York and London. It was a pile of bricks, carefully arranged into a rectangle on the gallery floor. Some declared it to be a work of utter genius. Others thought it looked rather like a pile of bricks. Each saw the same exhibit; the reactions and evaluations were dramatically different. The difference here is basically a matter of taste.

The cross is somewhat different. The difference can be understood from an illustration such as the following. Imagine two people standing together on the white cliffs of Dover in south-eastern England at some point in the period 26 May – 3 June 1941. Britain had declared war on Germany in September 1939. The Second World War had thus been going on for some time, and it had now entered into a crucial new phase. German armies had been moving westwards into France, driving all from their path. It seemed that little could stop them. British armies, attempting to resist this rapid advance, had been pinned down on the beaches of Dunkirk, a French coastal town just across the English channel from south-eastern England.

These two people standing on the cliffs would have seen lots of small boats coming and going from the local harbours. One of them might see nothing of note. All that seems to be happening is that lots of little boats are moving about. However, the other person sees exactly the same events, and yet is aware of a deeper and more significant truth linked to those same events, which the other observer misses. This second person knows that the little boats are engaged in the evacuation of the British Expeditionary Force from Dunkirk, and that the success of the operation holds the key to further resistance to Hitler, upon which the outcome of the Second World War would ultimately depend.

Both observers see the same events; one recognizes the crucial significance of what is going on, whereas the other does not. One, knowing the background to what is going on, knowing of the desperate situation in France on account of the astonishingly rapid German advance, recognizes that this a moment in history upon which much depends. The other sees nothing but the sea and some boats.

The same is true of the cross. Consider again the two people who might have been watching Jesus die on the cross at Calvary. One of them witnessed the death of a criminal. The other witnessed the saving death of the Son of God. Let us go back to our Dunkirk illustration for a moment. One observer noticed nothing more than lots of boats moving about in the English Channel. The other saw the salvation of what remained of the British Army and war effort. But which is right? The answer can only be that both are right, yet one is totally inadequate. The first is correct as far as it goes, but somehow manages to miss the entire point of the whole thing. So it is with the cross. One observer might notice a man dying on a cross; another sees God working out in a mysterious manner the salvation of the world, ourselves included.

The same sort of point can be seen in the parables of Jesus. When Jesus told parables, all those listening heard exactly the same words. All those around heard Jesus tell the parable of the prodigal son (Luke 15:11–32). Yet although everyone heard the same story about a boy who leaves home, only to return, two quite different understandings of and reactions to that story can be seen. Some heard a story about a boy who ran away from home, while others heard about the overwhelming and amazing love of God for sinners. One group heard the story, and missed its meaning; the other group heard exactly the same story, yet realized what it meant, and why it was such good news for repentant sinners. The gospels frequently point out how the crowds who heard the parables were puzzled by them; they had heard the words, but missed the meaning. So it is with the cross. To some, it is just about the death of a man. To others, it is about a loving God entering into the world to find and save us.

On 'being true' and 'being relevant'
On the basis of what has been said, it will be clear that the gospel is not about the mere historical facts that Jesus died and rose again; it is about what those events mean for sinners. We also need to appreciate that a careful distinction must be made between the truth and relevance of an event.

Something may be true, and yet quite without any real relevance. There will be few who will find themselves excited by the fact that the capital of the tiny nation of Albania is Tirana, or by the accuracy of the annual rainfall figures for the Scottish Highlands, or the exact type of gum used on the back of postage stamps issued by the British Virgin Islands between 1914–18. Facts are things which are true; they may also be deadly dull. 'Being true' doesn't necessarily mean 'being relevant'! In fact, something may be quite untrue, and enormously significant.

We can illustrate this by looking at events in the history of India, dating from the time when this region had been colonized and administered by the British. In the mid-1850s, new rifles were issued to soldiers of the East India Company. The old 'Brown Bess' was replaced with the Enfield rifle, which used a different type of cartridge. It was widely believed by the native Indian sepoys that the Enfield cartridges were greased with beef fat (which would be defiling to a Hindu) or pig fat (which would be defiling to a Muslim). As far as historical research can discover, this rumour does not appear to have been based upon fact; it was, however, enough to act as a major contributing cause to the Indian Mutiny of 1857, which came very close to forcibly ejecting the British from India. Although not true, it was certainly thought to be relevant to those who heard it!

With all these points about events and meanings, truth and relevance in mind, let us return to Paul's statements about the cross of Jesus Christ. It will be clear that Paul is making two important statements concerning the crucifixion: first, it is true; secondly, it is relevant. In other words, the event of the crucifixion really took place, and its significance is such that it has continuing relevance for us. The death of Jesus Christ is charged with significance. It is not simply an event from the past, as if it were limited to the pages of history textbooks. It is something which offers to change lives, bringing meaning and hope to the world.

So who is this man, through whom the Christian church has always claimed that we can have forgiveness of sins? Who is this man, whom Christians have worshipped as if he were God? What is so special about this man's death, that Christians celebrate it, where mourning might seem more appropriate? It is questions like these which come together under the two general areas of theology known as 'Christology' (that is, theories of the person of Christ) and 'soteriology' (that is, theories of what Christ achieved through his death upon the cross), and which we shall be considering in the remainder of this book. These two somewhat cumbersome technical terms will be used occasionally in the remainder of this work, but the reader need not feel under any obligation to use them. It is perfectly acceptable to speak of 'doctrines of the person of Christ' and 'doctrines of the work of Christ' instead.

So let us proceed immediately to discuss a question of major importance which underlies both these areas of Christian thought: why bother with doctrines anyway?

3

Why bother with doctrines about Jesus?

Theology is often regarded as idle and pointless speculation about irrelevancies – a harmless, if somewhat pointless, pastime of frustrated academics and bishops with time on their hands, with no real relevance to the business of everyday Christian living. If any area of Christian thought has been characterized by apparently pointless speculation of this sort, it is Christology (which is the technical term used by theologians to refer to theories concerning the person of Jesus Christ). The theologian Gregory of Nyssa, writing in the fourth century, complained that it was impossible to go out shopping in downtown Constantinople without having to put up with this kind of speculation:

> Constantinople is full of mechanics and slaves, every one of them profound theologians, who preach in the shops and streets. If you want someone to change a piece of silver, he tells you about how the Son differs from the Father; if you ask the price of a loaf of bread, you are told that the Son is inferior to the Father; if you ask

whether the bath is ready, you are told that the
Son was created from nothing.

Doctrine has got something of a bad name. So why
bother with it?

Why bother with doctrines?

There is a widespread feeling inside and outside the
Christian church today – as there always has been, and
probably always will be – that doctrines are a waste of
time. (The word 'doctrine' is generally used to mean 'a
Christian teaching'.) The Christian creeds all too often
appear as arid and dead formulas, bearing little relation
to the living faith of those who have to repeat them. It is
little cause for surprise that people find them of questionable value.

Take the case of someone who has a real and
profound experience of God. Perhaps they have just
come to faith, and have been overwhelmed by a sense of
the wonder of God, or an experience of the comfort of
his presence. Now imagine their reaction if they were to
compare this enormously rich and powerful experience
with the terse and bleak statements of the creeds of the
church. You can understand why someone like that
might feel that those creeds are more than a little petty,
pedantic and unreal in comparison! They will seem to be
totally incapable of capturing this experience, or
adequately reflecting it. How can the immensity, the
richness, the vitality and the sheer wonder of the Christian's experience of God in Christ be expressed in such
clumsy terms? Indeed, why bother with doctrines at all?
It is this question we must consider before going any
further, because inevitably we are going to end up with
doctrines about Jesus.

Doctrine and our experience of God

Christians are faced with something of a dilemma. On the one hand, they want to talk about God as the one who they experience, love and worship in adoration and wonder. On the other, they are only too painfully aware of the simple fact that God is God, and human language is quite incapable of adequately expressing everything which they would want to say about him. The words of the Psalmist are worth recalling: 'Be still, and know that I am God' (Psalm 46:10). The majesty and wonder of God tends to reduce us to silence. But we *must* speak of God, even though we recognize the inadequacy of our words to do justice either to God himself, or even to our experience of him.

I first studied theology at Oxford University, many years ago. One of my tutors was a distinguished Jesuit writer, based at Campion Hall, one of the many institutions of learning in Oxford. Each week, as I climbed the staircase leading to his room, I used to pass a gigantic oil painting of an elderly man and a young boy by the side of the sea. They were obviously engaged in some kind of conversation. Eventually, I asked someone to explain the painting, and was told the following story.

Augustine of Hippo, a celebrated theologian of the first great period of Christian thought, was writing a work which explored the Christian understanding of God. He was based in North Africa, in the region which is now modern-day Algeria. Perhaps he felt he needed a break; at any rate, he went for a walk along the coastline. As he was walking along the shore, he encountered a small boy pouring seawater into a hole in the sand. After emptying his pail of seawater into the hole, he would return to the sea, refill the pail, and repeat the process over again.

Augustine watched him for some time, and eventually asked him what he was doing. 'I'm pouring the Mediterranean Sea into this hole,' replied the boy. 'Don't be so stupid,' replied Augustine, 'you can't fit the sea into that little hole. You're wasting your time'. 'And so are you,' replied the boy, 'trying to write a book about God'. (It's one of those stories which, if it isn't true, certainly ought to be!) The boy was right: God cannot be squeezed into a book! There is just no way that human words can do justice to God.

But even with this sobering thought in mind, Augustine still felt it was important to try and speak about God, and inevitably to speak of him in terms of doctrines. In fact, it took centuries for the church to sort out the full significance of its experience of God and Christ, and express it (rather clumsily, some would say) in the doctrine of the Trinity. But it will be obvious that the Christian experience of God, Christ and the Holy Spirit was something common to Christian experience long before it was expressed in words or doctrines, or wrapped up in some sort of doctrinal formula. The experience of the presence of God, or the redeeming work of Christ, came first. Then the task began of making sense of it all. Who must Jesus be if he is able to redeem us? What must be true about him if we can experience him in our lives as our Saviour and Lord?

Doctrines and maps

In turning from our experience of God or Christ to doctrines about them, we are inevitably turning from one thing which is real and authentic to something else which is much less so. But this must be the case. An illustration may help explain why. Let us suppose that you cross the Atlantic from east to west on one of the

51

great ocean liners which used to ply their way from Europe to North America. Inevitably, you are overwhelmed by the sheer immensity of that ocean, and by the sense of being totally insignificant compared with its vastness. Your experience of the ocean makes a deep impression upon you, which you will naturally find difficult to express in words. However, you could still make a reasonable attempt at describing this experience to your friends.

Suppose that you then pick up a map of the western hemisphere, perhaps wanting to show your friends the route that the liner took. You will find Europe, North America and the Atlantic Ocean reduced to nothing more than some printed lines on a piece of paper. You may be fortunate enough to find the ocean coloured blue, and the land masses of America and Europe yellow - but all that you have in your hands is a piece of paper. How on earth does your experience of the Atlantic ocean relate to it?

Two points may be made. First, nobody in their right mind is going to suggest that the map is a substitute for the real thing. The map is not meant to be an exact replica of the Atlantic Ocean, in all its immensity and salty wetness, or the land mass of North America. Maps are, after all, meant to be manageable! The map is a representation, not a replica. It is an attempt to indicate how various things are related – for example, where Europe and America are situated in relation to each other. The map is not even meant to be a small model of the ocean, so that you can get the same sort of experience you once had, on a reduced scale. Rather, it is meant to convey certain limited (but important!) information, rather than reproduce an authentic experience. But if you wanted to reproduce your earlier experience, or help someone else to experience it, the map could be of vital importance, by indicating how you would achieve this.

Secondly, the map is based upon the personal experience of countless others, as they also crossed the Atlantic. Whereas your experience is undoubtedly real and important to you, it represents a single, isolated and very personal impression of a much greater reality. Taken on its own, your experience of the Atlantic ocean is unreliable, perhaps providing your friends with as much information about you as about the ocean itself. The function of the map is to combine as many impressions of a greater reality as possible, in order that a more reliable picture may be built up. The other experiences upon which the map is based are just as vivid and real as yours, but the map eliminates the *personal* element of experience of the Atlantic ocean, in order to provide a more generally reliable guide to the same reality.

The parallels between doctrines and maps will be obvious. First, a doctrine about Jesus was never meant to be a substitute for experience of him. It is simply an attempt to state something limited (but important!) about him, to relate him to God and to humanity, as the map relates the Atlantic Ocean to Europe and America. Thus the doctrine of the incarnation, as we shall see, makes it clear that Jesus Christ is the only mediator between God and ourselves. If we want to experience God fully and authentically, we will have to do so in and through Christ. Just as the map makes clear that you cannot travel westwards from Europe to North America without crossing the Atlantic, so the doctrine makes it clear that you cannot come to God without going through Jesus Christ.

Imagine how important this insight could be. Many people have been deeply moved by archive film from the early twentieth century, showing refugees leaving hopeless situations in Europe to make new lives in the United States. They knew that their hope of a new life lay in crossing the Atlantic Ocean. The map told them what to do if they were to find new life. The deep sense of relief and joy when the New York skyline came into view is well known to us through those films. And so it is with those who are seeking for God, for meaning and hope, in a seemingly dark, meaningless and hopeless world. Through Christ, they encounter the living God, the source of their new life, their hope and their joy. Doctrines about Jesus tell us how to find new life through him.

Again, many stories emerged from occupied Europe during the Second World War. Many of them concern the way in which prisoners of war managed to escape from the camps in which they had been imprisoned, such as Colditz. Their hope of escape and final freedom often rested on maps, which would guide them through the dark, impenetrable forests or across the great plains of Germany to find safety in countries such as Switzerland. Doctrines about Jesus Christ allow human beings who are imprisoned by sin to discover how to break free, and enter into the 'glorious liberty of the children of God' (Romans 8:21).

Sometimes those escape maps warned of dangers which could lead to recapture. Some doctrines fall into this category. For example, the doctrine of justification by faith signposts a false route. It tells us that we are unable to break free from sin by our own efforts; we must turn instead to trust in the grace of God. Sometimes the maps would identify things that needed to be done to cross

54

borders to reach safety. There are doctrines in this category as well. For example, the doctrine of salvation emphasizes that we must make a personal response to Christ if we are to benefit from all that he has done for us, and receive the 'benefits of Christ' (to use a helpful phrase from the sixteenth-century German writer, Philip Melanchthon).

Nobody is for one moment suggesting that this is everything that could be said about Jesus Christ, or that such doctrines adequately describe the deep personal significance which he holds for each and every believer. Nevertheless, doctrine does help us to begin to locate that significance, to be more precise about it than would otherwise be possible about how we encounter Christ, and what that implies for the transformation of our existence.

We all experience Jesus in a different way. He is seen through many eyes, and loved in many hearts. Inevitably, our attempts to describe this experience are going to be highly impressionistic, probably conveying more information about ourselves than about Jesus. Our backgrounds, our hopes and fears, our understanding of the world – all these things colour our impressions of Jesus. But when countless such experiences are taken into account, the individualist element may be eliminated. We are dealing with the cumulative experience of Christians as a whole. This allows us a more reliable account of the significance of Jesus, rather than the possibly confused impressions of a few individuals. Doctrines are essentially the distillation of the Christian experience of God, in which countless personal experiences are compared and reduced to their common features. It's not just my experience of God we're talking about; it is the common experience of the people of God down the ages.

Two aspects of faith

Christianity holds together two aspects of our experience of God. Although each of these aspects is important, each is inadequate on its own. On the one hand there is a purely emotional faith, which experiences God and trusts implicitly in him, but is unable to express itself coherently. We need to realize that faith has a content as well as an object. We don't just believe *in* God, we believe certain definite things about him. It is the task of every generation in the history of the Christian church to develop an articulate and authoritative account of its faith. Believers are also thinkers, and can never permit their faith to remain or become a shallow uninformed emotionalism. Emotion is an important element of the Christian faith, and those who despise it have no right to do so. On its own, however, it is inadequate, incapable of doing justice to the essence of Christian faith.

On the other hand, Christianity is not just a list of intellectual propositions or correct beliefs about God to which our assent is demanded. It is about personal experience of that same God. Christian belief in the divinity of Christ did not arise as an intellectual theory, but through the impact of experiencing redemption through him, and through him alone. The early Christians were faced with the intellectual task of thinking through the implications of their experience of Christ as God, and expressing it in as clear and persuasive a manner as possible.

Furthermore, it is possible for Christianity to degenerate into concern for an intellectual system, rather than for a person, who enters into our experience and transforms it. The intellectual side of Christian faith is important; on its own, however, it is inadequate. We need to preserve both the objective and subjective aspects of faith. Christian faith relates to both reason and experience. It is grounded in experience, but its content may still be summarized in propositions such as 'Jesus is Lord', 'Jesus is the Son of God', or 'Jesus is true God and true man'. There is no inconsistency involved – both the proposition and the experience relate to the same underlying reality. Faith involves both head and heart!

Why did doctrines develop?

It is interesting to reflect on the reason why the Christian church started laying down doctrines in the first place. It cannot be emphasized too strongly that doctrines are not a set of arbitrary regulations invented by some committee with nothing better to do. Far from it. In fact, doctrines were hammered out at moments when the very heart of the Christian faith seemed to be under threat through simplification, distortion or misunderstanding. They were needed to safeguard the very heart of the Christian faith, when misunderstandings or misrepresentations threatened to wreck its vital nature. The noted British crime fiction writer Dorothy L. Sayers, creator of Lord Peter Wimsey and also a fine theological writer, put this point as follows:

> Teachers and preachers never, I think, make it sufficiently clear that dogmas are not a set of arbitrary regulations invented *a priori* by a committee of theologians enjoying a bout of all-in dialectical wrestling. Most of them were hammered out under pressure or urgent practical necessity to provide an answer to heresy.

Christian doctrines and dogmas became inevitable when disagreement arose within the church about what the

Christian experience of God and Christ actually meant. There was every danger that an understanding of God or Christ would arise which made some sort of sense intellectually, but could not do justice to the richness of the Christian experience of God. It was much simpler to believe that Jesus was just a splendid example of humanity, with insights and abilities denied to most of us, than to believe that he was (in some sense of the word) God. The difficulty was that this simply didn't seem to tie in with either the biblical witness to Christ, or with the way in which Christians experienced him as present in their lives. It might be simple, but it didn't have the 'ring of truth'.

Some words of the Anglo-American poet T. S. Eliot are worth considering here: 'We had the experience, but missed the meaning, but approach to the meaning restored the experience'. Doctrine cannot be isolated from Christian worship and prayer. Christians worship, adore and pray to Jesus Christ – practices which make no sense if Jesus was just a good religious teacher. This simpler, neater, more attractive approach to Jesus was simply inconsistent with the fact that Christians worshipped and adored him, prayed to him, and experienced him in a personal manner. Doctrines about Jesus aim to be faithful both to Scripture and to the Christian experience of God and the risen Christ. Once rival theories of Jesus' identity and significance began to appear (such as Arianism, an early heresy which denied the divinity of Christ), which were so obviously deficient in this respect, the church had to make some sort of response.

So doctrines were hammered out, and expressed in creeds. They were never meant to be a substitute for Christian experience. Rather, they were a kind of 'hedge', marking out an area of thought about God and Christ which seemed to be faithful to Christian experience on the one hand, and Scripture on the other. 'If the Arians had won, Christianity would have dwindled to a legend' (Thomas Carlyle). Experience and meaning would have drifted apart, eventually to the point where both were lost. It is simply not true that doctrine is a hopeless irrelevance to the life and work of the Christian church. It is one of the few safeguards by which its identity and relevance have been, and still are preserved in the face of a disbelieving world.

Jesus as just a good religious teacher?

There is still a widespread reluctance in some quarters to allow Jesus Christ any claim to be God in any meaningful sense of the word. The popular idea of Christianity is still that Jesus Christ was a great moral teacher, and that everyone would get along much better if they took his advice seriously. Of course, there have been other outstanding teachers before Jesus and after him, such as Plato, Aristotle, Confucius, and so on. The popular idea of Christianity is that Jesus is just like these teachers. If there is any difference between him and them, it is one of degree, rather than kind. They are all basically human beings, enlightened to various degrees, who have contributed to (or at least tried to contribute to) the moral education of humanity.

The first difficulty with this view is that it is only too painfully obvious that we have never really tended to pay much advice to teachers. We have had plenty of good moral advice over the last three or four thousand years, and that given by Jesus is unlikely to make much difference if it isn't followed. Indeed, we might go further and suggest that there appears to be something about human nature which makes it impossible to benefit from good advice, so that more than education is required if our situation is to be altered for the better.

But there is a more serious difficulty. Christians simply do not view Jesus in this way. They do not treat Jesus Christ as yet another religious teacher. That would be to make Jesus a rabbi, where Christians speak of him as their Lord and Saviour. They talk about Jesus being the 'Bread of Life', or the 'Lamb of God, who takes away the sin of the world'. They will undoubtedly make reference to – and value! – Jesus' moral teaching, but their main interest concerns the significance of his death and resurrection. Just as with Paul, interest in the crucified and risen Christ has almost completely overshadowed his teaching ministry. Good teachers, after all, are not that difficult to find; people who are crucified, only to be raised from the dead, are somewhat fewer on the ground, and command attention for that very reason.

Christians have never looked back to revere the memory of a dead teacher, but have looked up to worship a living Lord. However difficult the terms may be, the fact is that Christians have tended to designate the crucified and risen Jesus as 'Lord', 'Son of God' or 'Saviour', and have gathered together on the day of the week marking his resurrection to worship him as their Saviour and Lord, rather than just learn from him as their teacher. The Communion Service is not a solemn memorial of the death of a great teacher or leader, but the celebration of Christ's saving death and resurrrection by those whom he has redeemed.

We can learn much from the history of the Christian church in the first few centuries of its existence, not least that the early Christians had no hesitation in worshipping Christ as God. This practice was noted by the younger Pliny in his famous letter of AD 112 to the

Emperor Trajan, in which he reports that Christians sang hymns to their Lord 'as God' (*quasi deo*). The views of one early maverick theologian, to the effect that Christ was merely a rather special man, was answered with an appeal to the universal Christian practice of singing 'psalms and songs written from the beginning by faithful brethren, which celebrate the Word of God, that is Christ, and speak of him as God'. The heretic bishop Paul of Samosata, deposed in 268, attempted to stop his congregations worshipping Christ, recognizing that this well-established practice, which continues to the present day, posed an irrefutable challenge to his own view that Christ was not divine (in any meaningful sense of the word).

The Arian controversy of the early fourth century served to highlight these points. Arius, while giving Christ precedence over all of God's creatures, insisted that he was still nothing more than a creature, rather than God. Although Jesus was to be treated as the first among men, he was still a man, and nothing more than a man. Two major lines of argument were advanced against him by his orthodox opponent Athanasius. First, he repeated the point we have just noted. Arius, he suggested, was making the entire church guilty of worshipping a creature, rather than God. Only God could be worshipped, argued Athanasius, and as Christians had worshipped Christ from the beginning of the Christian era, this meant that Christ had to be regarded as divine.

We are dealing with two quite different, yet closely related questions here. One is the question of the identity of Jesus: who is he? The other is the question of the function of Jesus: what does he do? But these are closely related. To say that Jesus is the Saviour of the world is to establish his function (in other words, what he does: he saves). But who must Jesus be if he is able to act in this way? What must we say about his identity on the basis of this specific function? After all, the only one who could save us is God. Therefore, if Jesus saves us, he must be God. Beginning from Jesus' function, his identity was deduced.

The argument can also be used the other way round, working from Jesus' identity to his function. It could be argued that Jesus was God (which is a statement about his identity). Therefore, it is argued, Jesus must reveal God (which is a statement about his function). For our purposes, it doesn't matter which way round this is argued: the point we want to make is that Jesus' identity and significance are closely related. In establishing who Jesus *is*, we have to bear in mind what he *does*.

For Paul, Jesus was the bearer of salvation to sinners: the 'benefits of Christ' were the forgiveness of sins, reconciliation to God, and the hope of resurrection. To 'know Christ' involves recognizing his significance for us - in other words, recognizing the 'benefits' which he brings, making them our own, and subsequently reflecting on who Jesus must be if he is able to do this for us.

This kind of argument became important during the Arian controversy. Athanasius, Arius' most vigorous opponent, argued that Jesus was worshipped by Christians, which established his function as one who was worshipped. But who must Jesus be if he can be worshipped in this way? Athanasius argued that only one who is God can be worshipped, in that only God is entitled to worship. We can see here an argument from Christ's function (as an object of worship) to his identity (as God, who alone may be worshipped). Athanasius followed this up by pointing out that created beings cannot be saved by another created being. Only God can save, and as Christ saves us (which Arius did not, incidentally, dispute), he must be treated as God. Once more, we can see a direct argument from Christ's function (as Saviour) to his identity (as God).

The early Christians, then, worshipped Christ as a fully divine Saviour, regarding this as the obvious interpretation of the New Testament material. This basic understanding of the identity and function of Jesus Christ has remained characteristic of Christianity since then, despite a number of challenges to this understanding from within, as well as outside of, the Christian church. One such challenge is particularly interesting, and is worth considering in some detail. This is the so-called 'Quest for the Historical Jesus', which culminated in the last century, noted earlier. In the following chapter, however, we shall consider the nature of the New Testament sources. An understanding of the nature of those sources allows us to see these attempts to 'reconstruct' Jesus in a more realistic light.

4

The sources of our
knowledge of Jesus

We are almost totally dependent upon the New Testament, and particularly the first three gospels, for our knowledge about Jesus. Although there are early documents other than the New Testament writings which make reference to Jesus, or the beliefs of Christians about him, these are of little interest to any except specialist historians, and have no decisive importance for the Christian faith. Inevitably, every now and then a secular writer claims that one of these writings gives us information which totally discredits Christianity. No such claim has survived serious scholarly examination.

For some, the relative silence of such sources is a problem. After all, if Jesus was the Saviour of the world, you might well expect other historical sources from the first century to pay more attention to him! However, the situation is not that simple. Our main sources for a knowledge of any aspect of the first century are Roman historical writers. These writers cause some problems for historians, both because they are so few in number and their writings largely exist as fragments. And how could a secular historian, based in Rome, appreciate that some seemingly insignificant events in a backwater of the Roman Empire would lay the foundations for a major world religion? They may have been good historians, at least by the standards of their times; they were certainly not clairvoyants. They could hardly have foreseen that what seemed in the first century to be nothing more than an obscure Palestinian sect, yet another splinter group within a half-understood Judaism, would one day come to dominate the Roman Empire, let alone much of the civilized world!

It must be appreciated that Judea was a backwater of the Roman empire, to which nobody paid much attention in the first place. Furthermore, thousands of Jewish agitators were crucified in Judea under the Romans: one more would have passed unnoticed. In fact, we find exactly what we might expect: Roman historians pay no attention to Christianity at all, except when it causes social or political disturbances in the city of Rome itself. Events in distant Palestine were deemed irrelevant to the writing of Roman history. Even where Roman historians make reference to Christianity's growing appeal in Rome, their chief interest concerns the disturbances it caused, rather than the beliefs of Christians.

Having said that, we find reference to Jesus in four classical authors of the first or early second centuries. These are: 1. Thallus, a first century Greek writer with a particular interest in relating Roman history to the history of the eastern Mediterranean, cited by Julius Africanus in the third century; 2. Pliny the Younger, writing at some point around AD 111 to Trajan, detailing the rapid spread of Christianity in Asia Minor (modern-day Turkey); 3. Tacitus, who wrote around AD 115 concerning the momentous events of AD 64, in which the emperor Nero made Christians the scapegoats for the burning of Rome; 4. Suetonius, writing at some point around AD 120 concerning certain events in the reign of the emperor Claudius. Suetonius refers to a certain 'Chrestus' who he believed to have been behind recent rioting at Rome. It should be remembered that 'Christus' was still an unfamiliar name to Romans at this stage, whereas 'Chrestus' was a common name for slaves (meaning 'someone who is useful'). Even in the third and fourth centuries, Christian writers were still complaining about people who mis-spelled 'Christus' as 'Chrestus'.

What do these pagan authors tell us about Jesus? Not as much as we would like. Nevertheless, it is clear that we can draw some useful conclusions from their writings. 1. Tacitus reports that Christ had been condemned to death by Pontius Pilate, procurator of Judea, during the reign of the Roman emperor Tiberius. Pilate was procurator of Judea from AD 26–36, while Tiberius reigned from AD 14–37. The traditional date for the crucifixion is around AD 30–33. 2. Thallus reports that, at the time of the crucifixion, there seems to have been some sort of supernatural darkness, which some explained in terms of a total eclipse of the sun. 3. By the time of Nero, Christ had attracted sufficient followers in Rome to make them a suitable scapegoat for the burning of Rome. According to Tacitus, these followers were named 'Christians' after him. 4. Suetonius tells his readers that this mysterious 'Chrestus' was the founder of a distinctive sect within Judaism. 5. Pliny reported that Christians worshipped Jesus as if he were God, abandoning the worship of the Roman emperor to do so, and thus risking execution under the severe laws of the period.

These historical details tie in well with the New Testament accounts. Fragmentary though they are, they are remarkably consistent with the New Testament witness.

The nature of the gospels

What sort of documents are the gospels? In an earlier chapter, we saw that the 'Quest for the Historical Jesus' movement believed it was possible to sift through Christian beliefs about Jesus and find the 'real' Jesus who lay behind them. It was argued that Christianity had got Jesus wrong; it was time to get him right! One of the assumptions made by the movement was that the gospels, particularly the Synoptic Gospels (that is, Matthew, Mark and Luke) could be treated as historical sources. In other words, the gospels were treated as if they were completely impartial documents, which merely recorded facts (rather than opinions) about Jesus. It was then up to the individual reader of the gospels to make sense of these facts as best he could.

In practice most of those engaged in the 'Quest for the Historical Jesus' found themselves, like Nelson, turning a blind eye to those facts recorded in the gospels which they found awkward. Their desire to discover a simple moral teacher in Jesus led them to ignore or explain away certain events recorded by the gospels which didn't fit their preconceived pattern. For example, the gospel accounts of Jesus' resurrection clearly imply that he was infinitely more than a wandering Jewish moralist. These were ignored or rationalized as misunderstandings. Similarly, the gospel accounts of Jesus' awareness of the saving power of his forthcoming death at the hands of the leaders of his own people were also something of an embarrassment, and were thus passed over in much the same way. The real significance of Jesus, according to this movement, was his teaching, particularly as expressed in the Sermon on the Mount and the parables. Jesus was thus turned into little more than a stereotype – the religious teacher. Those elements of his ministry which did not conform to this straitjacket were explained away, ignored or suppressed.

But this ignores a whole series of crucial questions: why were the gospels written in the first place? How can we explain the way in which the material is arranged within the gospels? What factors determined the material which was included in the gospels? All too often, the scholars of the nineteenth century seem to have assumed that the gospels were written for *their* convenience, a collection of sayings of Jesus which *they* could interpret as they pleased. If something didn't appeal to the reinterpreters of Jesus, they felt able to pass over it or explain it away. They already knew what was right; any 'evidence' which inconveniently got in the way of these preconceived conclusions was simply sidelined. All too often, the theory dictated the conclusion in advance of the evidence.

Since the last years of the nineteenth century, however, it has become clear that the gospels simply cannot be treated in this slapdash and superficial way. The first three gospels are indeed reliable sources for knowledge of Jesus; that point has been confirmed, rather than called into question, by responsible New Testament scholarship. (Sensationalizing works declaring otherwise will always hit the headlines, while the serious and responsible work of New Testament scholarship works on, unnoticed, in the background.) What has become increasingly clear is that this knowledge takes a particular form, which cannot be ignored when it comes to interpreting it.

The gospels were not written by Jesus himself, nor do they date from his lifetime. It is generally thought that Jesus was crucified around the years AD 30–33, and that the earliest gospel (probably Mark) dates from about AD 65. There is probably a gap of about thirty years between the events described in the gospels taking place, and subsequently being written down in the form of a gospel. By classical standards, this was an incredibly short time. The Buddha, for example, had one thing in common with Jesus: he wrote nothing down. Yet the definitive collection of his sayings (the 'Tripitaka') is thought to date from around four centuries after his death – more than ten times the interval between the death of Jesus and the appearance of the first gospel.

In any case, Christians were committed to writing down their understanding of the importance of Jesus long before Mark's gospel was written. The New Testament letters (still sometimes referred to as the 'epistles') date mainly from the period AD 49–69, and provide confirmation of the importance and interpretations of Jesus in this formative period. It is now becoming clear that Paul's letters include many references to the teaching of Jesus, providing an important link between the epistles and the gospels.

Yet despite these comments, some readers may find this gap of thirty years distressing. Why were these things not written down immediately? Might people not forget what Jesus said and did, and what happened at the crucifixion and resurrection? Yet this overlooks the fact that Christians were preaching the good news of Jesus to the world from within weeks of his resurrection, making full use of this material. There was no danger of forgetting about Jesus; his words and deeds were constantly being recalled by Christian preachers and evangelists.

It is difficult for twentieth century readers, who are so used to information being recorded in written or other visual form, to appreciate that the classical world communicated by means of the spoken word. The great Homeric epics are good examples of the way in which stories were passed on with remarkable accuracy from one generation to another. If there is one ability which modern westerners have probably lost, it is the ability to remember a story or narrative as it is told, and then to pass it on to others afterwards.

As one study of primitive culture after another confirms, the passing down of stories from one generation to another was characteristic of the pre-modern era, including the time of the New Testament itself. Indeed, there are excellent grounds for arguing that early educational systems were based upon learning by rote. The fact that most people in the West today find it difficult to commit even a short story or narrative to memory naturally tends to prejudice them against believing that anyone else could do it; yet it is evident that it was done, and was done remarkably well. Yet this ability has not been completely lost. I remember a friend, who was a university lecturer in ancient history at Oxford, once describing his astonishment when an elderly Jew who he knew was able to recite the entire Old Testament in Hebrew from memory, while being checked against the printed text!

The period between the death of Jesus and the writing of the first gospel is usually referred to as the 'period of oral tradition', meaning the period in which accounts of Jesus' birth, life and death, as well as his teaching, were passed down with remarkable accuracy from one generation to another. In this period, it seems that certain of Jesus' sayings, and certain aspects of his life, especially his death and resurrection, were singled out as being of particular importance, and were passed down from the first Christians to those who followed them. Others were not passed down, and have been lost forever. The early Christians seem to have identified what was essential, and what was not so important, of Jesus' words, deeds and fate, and passed down only the former to us.

An excellent example of this process of oral transmission may be found in Paul's first letter to the Christians at Corinth, almost certainly dating from the period of oral transmission:

For I received from the Lord what I also passed on to you: The Lord Jesus, on the night he was betrayed, took bread, and when he had given thanks, he broke it and said, 'This is my body, which is for you; do this in remembrance of me.' In the same way, after supper he took the cup, saying, 'This cup is the new covenant in my blood; do this, whenever you drink it, in remembrance of me.' (1 Corinthians 11:23–25).

Paul is here passing something on to the Corinthian Christians which had been passed on to him, presumably by word of mouth. It is interesting to compare these verses with their equivalents in the gospels (Matthew 26:26–28; Mark 14:22–24; Luke 22:17–19.)

The 'period of oral tradition' may thus be regarded as a period of 'sifting', in which the first Christians

71

assessed what was necessary to pass down to those who followed them. Thus Jesus' sayings may have become detached from their original context, and perhaps on occasion even given a new one, simply through the use to which the first Christians put them – proclaiming the gospel to those outside the early community of faith, and deepening and informing the faith of those inside it.

There is every reason to suppose that those early Christians preserved and transmitted faithfully the *substance* and the *meaning* of Jesus' teaching and actions, even if it is conceivable that some slight differences in the precise wording of Jesus' sayings, or the chronology of his actions, may have arisen. The early Christians were preachers, not parrots. Although the gospel writers did pass on to their readers authentic traditions concerning Jesus, those traditions were selected on the basis of the needs of the early Christian church, as it sought to spread the gospel. Perhaps John's gospel states this point most clearly:

> Jesus did many other miraculous signs in the presence of his disciples, which are not recorded in this book. But these are written that you may believe that Jesus is the Christ, the Son of God, and that by believing you may have life in his name (John 20:30–31).

This passage states two things explicitly. First, it identifies the principle of *selectivity*. The gospel writers have been selective in their material (note also John 21:25), following the oral tradition passed down to them. Much information about Jesus has been lost forever, simply because the early Christians did not feel that it was of any relevance to their purposes of evangelization and teaching. Secondly, it explains the motivation underlying the writing of the gospels. They were written with the purpose of conversion in mind. Their purpose was to generate and inform faith on the part of their readers. To develop this point, we must return to the distinction between event and interpretation.

As we noted earlier, Christianity is not concerned principally with the events associated with Jesus Christ, but with the interpretation of the significance of those events. The gospel writers were not concerned primarily with recording the events of the life and death of Jesus, but with indicating their significance. They mingle history and interpretation, in that they both record and indicate the significance of events. Thus in the passage quoted above from John's gospel, the evangelist (as the writers of the gospel are known) is clearly drawing a distinction between 'signs' (events) and 'believing that Jesus is the Christ, the Son of God' (interpretation). Similarly, we find Paul appealing to an oral tradition which combines the report of events (Jesus' death and resurrection) with the interpretation of these events (forgiveness of sins) at 1 Corinthians 15:3–5.

Clues to the identity of Jesus

Let us now return to the Synoptic Gospels (Matthew, Mark and Luke), and look more closely at the way they portray Christ. The gospels are not biographies, although they do indeed contain a hard core of historical information about Jesus. Nor are they religious textbooks, spelling out the basics of Christian ethics, although they do contain much teaching concerning morality. Perhaps the most helpful way of thinking of them is to draw a parallel with a totally different type of modern literary form – the detective novel.

The essence of every good detective novel lies in engaging the reader in the detective's search for the murderer. In effect, we are set alongside the fictional detective, as he or she discovers clues, and gradually builds up a picture of what must have happened, in order to uncover the identity of the murderer in an exciting climax. It is only at this point that we readers find out whether we have noticed all the clues, and worked out their significance. Of course, there is always something of a temptation for the author of such novels to introduce so many 'red herrings' that it is difficult to distinguish them from real clues. Certain novelists (such as Agatha Christie) have even been known to conceal clues from their readers in order to hold their interest to the final chapter.

Now there is one obvious difference between the gospels and crime fiction: the gospels are not fiction! As I have emphasized, the gospels are about real history – a history with a saving significance, yet firmly grounded in the bedrock of real historical events. In other respects, however, there are some helpful analogies between the gospels and this type of writing. The reader of the gospels is set alongside the disciples as they listen to Jesus preach, watch him in action, and finally see him die and raised again. Just as mystery writers allow their readers to follow them in their action of searching for clues, so the gospel writers set their readers alongside Jesus. We are allowed to discover the clues which they discovered, and share their puzzlement over what they might mean.

But whereas detective novels are basically 'Whodunits', the gospels are 'Whowasits'. They are interested in establishing the identity and significance of their central figure, rather than with picking out a murderer from a number of possible suspects. The gospel writers allow us to see and hear what the disciples heard, and force us to ask much the same questions which they must have asked before us. What do these things mean? Who is this man? And just as the writers of detective novels single out, or draw our attention to, significant things (in other words, clues) which we might otherwise have overlooked, so the gospel writers do the same. Before considering some examples, an important point needs to be made.

It is easy to overlook clues. Something may take place which appears to be insignificant at the time, and yet assumes a much greater significance later, as its full meaning becomes obvious. Arthur Conan Doyle's story *Silver Blaze*, which tells of how the great fictional detective Sherlock Holmes investigates an attack on a valuable racehorse, is a case in point. The full significance of the fact that the watchdog did not bark during the night only becomes evident at a late stage. The fact was observed, but its significance only becomes apparent later, when Holmes points out that it could only mean that the dog knew the intruder. Conan Doyle thus had to single out this one apparently insignificant fact (and ignore other apparently equally insignificant facts) because it would later be of vital importance. He has to be selective, 'filtering' out facts which he knows (on account of later developments) to be important, and igoring others, which he knows are not so important (even though this may not have been obvious at the time at which they took place).

There is every reason to suppose that something similar has happened in the gospels, where the fact that something did *not* happen is often important. Mark notes that Jesus was silent before his accusers (Mark 14·61), where he might have been expected to defend himself. The significance of this silence can be seen in the light of the silence of the Suffering Servant (Isaiah 53:7) before his accusers. Mark appears to want us to pick up this clue, and draw us on to note other parallels between Jesus and this mysterious Old Testament figure.

The first Christians appear to have realized the full significance of some of the things which Jesus said or did only after his resurrection, when they suddenly saw things in a completely new light. An apparently insignificant fact assumed a new meaning, simply because its full significance was realized – perhaps late in the day, but better late than never. Thus in John's gospel, Jesus makes a remark which appears to refer to the temple at Jerusalem; after the resurrection, however, his disciples realized that it referred to Jesus himself (John 2:18–22). Some clues were impossible to overlook – the resurrection itself being the most obvious example. Others were more subtle, and were only recognized for what they really were after the resurrection, when the penny finally dropped for the disciples. This serves to remind us that the gospel accounts are meant to be read in the light of faith in the resurrection, which the early Christians took as fundamental to their beliefs about Jesus.

The gospel witness to Jesus Christ

So what conclusions do the gospel writers want us to draw? Matthew initially wants us to recognize that Jesus was the Messiah, the long-awaited descendant of King David who was expected to usher in a new era in the history of Israel. The first part of his gospel is therefore littered with clues pointing to this conclusion. The gospel opens with a list of Jesus' forebears (Matthew 1:1–17) which establishes that Jesus was legally the son of David, as the Messiah was expected to be. In his account of the birth of Jesus, Matthew makes sure that we don't overlook the remarkable parallels between the circumstances of that birth and the prophecies of the Old Testament, drawing our attention to this point no less than five times in his first two chapters (Matthew 1:22–23; 2:5–6; 2:16; 2:17–18; 2:23).

Mark's gospel opens by establishing the credentials of John the Baptist. John is the long-expected messenger who prepares the way for the coming of the Lord (Mark 1:2–3). Having established this, Mark records John the Baptist's statement that someone even more significant will come after him (Mark 1:7–8). And who is it who comes on to the scene at once? 'At that time Jesus came from Nazareth in Galilee and was baptized by John in the Jordan' (Mark 1:9). The conclusion Mark wishes us to draw is obvious.

Although some of the clues concerning the identity and significance of Jesus are pointed out with some force, others are left to readers to pick up for themselves. For example, Jesus regularly addresses God as 'Father' in his prayers – a very presumptuous practice by the standards of the time. At one point, Mark even gives us the Aramaic original of the word for 'Father' – *Abba*, a remarkably familiar term impossible to translate into English ('Papa', 'Dad', 'Daddy', often being suggested as the nearest equivalents). The gospel writers do not bring out the full significance of this practice, which clearly points to Jesus understanding himself to have a very intimate relationship to God. It is left to their readers to spot this point, and appreciate the importance of their discovery. Every educationalist knows the importance of allowing people to make their own discoveries; the gospel writers are no exception!

Equally, the remarkable parallels between the 'Righteous Sufferer' of Psalm 22 and the accounts of Christ's passion are not made explicit, but are left unsaid. Jesus' words 'My God, my God, why have you forsaken me?' (Matthew 27:46) – the only point, incidentally, at which Jesus does not address God as 'Father' – draw our attention to this mysterious Psalm, and particularly to its descriptions of the mode of death of the 'Righteous Sufferer'. This figure is mocked by those who watch him die (Psalm 22:6–8), as is Jesus (Matthew 27:39–44). He has his hands and feet pierced (Psalm 22:16), as would most victims of crucifixion, including Jesus. He sees his tormentors casting lots for his clothes (Psalm 22:18), as does Jesus (Matthew 27:35).

Another remarkable parallel exists between the crucifixion and the account of the 'Suffering Servant' of Isaiah 53, which only Luke notes explicitly (Luke 22:37). This famous Old Testament prophecy speaks of a Suffering Servant of God, who was 'pierced for our transgressions' and 'crushed for our iniquities' (Isaiah 53:5). Perhaps the most significant part of this prophecy relates to the fact that the servant is 'numbered with the transgressors' (Isaiah 53:12), which is clearly understood by the gospel writers to be paralleled in two manners. First, Christ died by crucifixion, which, as we emphasized in Chapter 2, was a mode of death reserved for criminals. In other words, Christ was identified with sinners by the manner of his death. Secondly, Christ was not crucified alone, but along with two criminals (Matthew 27:38). In both ways, Christ's death was realized to parallel that of an important Old Testament figure. Other parallels with this account may be seen in the gospels, although they are not pointed out by the gospel writers. Luke notes that Jesus prayed for his executioners (Luke 23:34), paralleling the actions of the Suffering Servant (Isaiah 53:12). In fact, it seems that the first Christians could not help but notice the obvious parallels between the life and death of Jesus and certain significant prophecies of the Old Testament, and take a certain degree of delight in pointing them out to their readers, or allowing them to discover them for themselves.

Seeing the overall picture

The evangelists were theologians, rather than just biographers, painting a portrait of Jesus which attempted to bring out the full richness of their impressions of him. When looking at a painting, such as a landscape, we can concentrate our attention upon one part of it, examining the small detail underlying the artist's work. The great portrayal of a Flemish landscape may, on closer examination, disclose astonishing attention to detail in individual blades of grass. But it is the overall impression which the picture conveys which is of crucial importance. After marvelling at the landscape, our attention may wander to consider the intricacy of the artwork on the blades of grass, as one component of that landscape. But it is the overall impression and impact which really count.

It is the same with Jesus. It is the overall impression which counts, rather than the fine details which make it up. Jesus was experienced by the disciples as a living person, a totality rather than a sum of small parts. Later, as the first Christians reflected on the astonishing personality of Jesus, they were able to discriminate between the various elements which contributed to the impression he made upon them. But this is something which happened later, after the passage of time allowed such an analysis to take place. The immediate impression which Jesus made upon those whom he encountered is what underlies this analysis. What was it about Jesus that caused those fishermen to drop their nets, leave everything, and follow him into the unknown? What was it that caused people to marvel at his teaching? With remarkable skill, the evangelists paint for us a portrait of Christ as the King of Israel, the Servant of the Lord, the Friend of Sinners and the Word Incarnate.

No single human witness to Jesus could ever encompass the totality of his person, just as no single person could ever hope to depict him definitively. The gospels preserve a collection of memories and interpretations of Jesus which Christians recognized to be authentic, building up to give a portrait of Jesus Christ as Saviour and Lord. This was not done in some clumsy or haphazard way, like a child cutting up bits of paper and pasting them into a scrapbook, but by a genuinely creative and inspired process, in which material was brought together in the mind of the evangelist as a consistent whole. It is this consistent portrayal of Christ which finds its expression in the gospels. Behind the wealth of detail which we find in the gospels lies an attempt to express the totality of Jesus Christ. The details are like brush-strokes, which build up to form a portrait. Each such brush-stroke, taken on its own, is inadequate to disclose the whole vision of the painter. But taken together, they form an impression of the person sitting in front of the artist.

There is every danger that, as we study the gospels, we will fail to see the wood for the trees, the portrait for the brush-strokes, the landscape for the blades of grass. If we look at a television screen very closely, we can see that the picture is made up of very small coloured dots. But to see the picture on that screen, we have to stand back, losing sight of this fine detail, as the dots merge to form a picture. In much the same way, we must learn to stand back from the small details of Jesus, in order to grasp him as a whole. Christ thus emerges as Saviour and Lord. We will overlook the portrayal of Christ as Saviour and Lord if we concentrate upon only one aspect of his life or ministry, such as the parables or the passion narratives. We must learn to see these as pieces of a jigsaw, as intricate detail in a work of art, all combining to disclose Jesus to us as he once disclosed himself to his disciples. There is far more to Jesus than any of us can ever fully appreciate.

The gospels portray the gradual dawn of faith in the disciples. Initially, they see in Jesus a great teacher – someone who taught with authority, unlike their own teachers (Mark 1:27). Gradually, other insights begin to develop: for example, Jesus performs signs and wonders which arouse enormous popular interest in him throughout the region. Eventually, they have sufficient information at their disposal to come to the conclusion which marks a turning point in the gospel narratives: the confession that Jesus is the Messiah (Matthew 16:16; Mark 8:29; Luke 9:20). Once the disciples have achieved this basic insight, Jesus tells them that he must be rejected by his own people, suffer, be killed, and rise again (Matthew 16:21; Mark 8:31; Luke 9:22). The emphasis upon the fact that this *must* happen, and the use of the construction 'be killed', rather than simply 'die', indicates that the early Christians regarded Christ's death as an integral part of his ministry and mission. This fact is perfectly obvious from the remaining writings of the New Testament, most of which were written before the gospels, even if the gospels do not choose to emphasize it. The gospel writers probably assumed that their readers already knew this.

81

The first Christians simply did not regard Jesus' death as an untimely end to the promising career of a radical and innovative rabbi, but as one of the two culminating points of Jesus' mission (the other being his resurrection). Jesus' teaching, important and distinctive though it unquestionably is, assumes its full significance only through the recognition of who he is. To put it very crudely: if you have good reason to think that you are dealing with someone who may well be God incarnate, you are likely to take what that person says and does a lot more seriously than you otherwise would!

At this point, we have sufficient information at our disposal to begin looking seriously at the question of the identity and significance of Jesus. In the second part of this book, we shall look at the question of who Jesus is (often referred to in the technical literature as 'the doctrine of the person of Christ' or 'Christology'; in the third part, we shall examine the question of what Jesus' significance for us actually is (sometimes referred to in the technical literature as 'the doctrine of the work of Christ' or 'soteriology').

Part 2

The person of Jesus Christ

5

The resurrection

Why do Christians insist upon Jesus being far more than a good religious teacher? Why do they want to speak of him in terms of his being 'Saviour', 'Lord' or 'God'? There are many who would like Christians to abandon this practice. Many liberal Christian writers believe that inter-religious dialogue would be made a lot easier if Jesus Christ could be presented as the religious teacher of Christians, in much the same way as Mohammed is the prophet who makes God known for Muslims.

The doctrine, however, is non-negotiable. It is not a dispensable element of the Christian faith. It is there because it *has* to be there. There is no other way of doing justice to the New Testament witness to Christ, or to the realities of Christian experience down the centuries. It is not something over which we have control, to discard at will. It is something which is both essential and central to the Christian faith. The great British writer C. S. Lewis put it like this, in a letter to his friend Arthur Greeves, dated 11 December 1944:

> The doctrine of Christ's divinity seems to me not something stuck on which you can unstick but something that peeps out at every point so that

you'd have to unravel the whole web to get rid
of it.

For Lewis, the coherence of Christianity was such that it
was impossible to eliminate the idea of the divinity of
Christ without doing such damage to the web of Christian doctrine that the entire structure of the Christian
faith would collapse. Far from being an optional extra,
something which had accidentally been added and which
now required removal, it was an essential and integral
part of the authentically Christian understanding of
reality.

So what are the grounds of this belief, and why is it
so central to Christianity? Christianity would be a lot
simpler if Jesus was just a good religious teacher. Why
all this fuss about his divinity? What difference does it
make? Such questions *must* be asked, for it is only by
asking them that we are confronted with both the
theological foundations and the spiritual implications of
the basic Christian belief that Jesus is divine. Exploring
the grounds and consequences of the divinity of Christ
can be one of the most liberating and exciting pilgrimages which the Christian can hope to make. Let us begin
our exploration at the most obvious and appropriate
point: the resurrection of Jesus Christ.

The evidence for the resurrection

Paul opens his letter to the Christians at Rome by
making a crucially important statement concerning Jesus
Christ, who 'as to his human nature was a descendant of
David, and who through the Spirit of holiness was
declared with power to be the Son of God by his resurrection from the dead' (Romans 1:3–4). This brief statement picks out two reasons why Jesus is to be regarded

as the Son of God. First, on the physical level, he was a descendant of David, the great king of Israel to whom God had promised a future successor as king. A similar point is made by Matthew, as he opens his gospel (Matthew 1:1). Secondly, Jesus' resurrection established his identity as the Son of God. Paul assumes that the resurrection was a real historical event. The important thing for him is to establish what it means.

In the modern period, however, the suggestion that Jesus might have risen from the dead has been treated with intense scepticism by some. The resurrection, they argue, is at best a misunderstanding, and probably a total fabrication. Before we can ask what the resurrection means, we must establish that it took place at all. So let us begin by looking at the evidence.

The New Testament is dominated by the resurrection
The theme of the resurrection resonates throughout the New Testament, and in the preaching of the early church in the period after the completion of the New Testament writings. This obviously doesn't prove that the resurrection took place: what it does prove beyond any reasonable doubt is that the first generations of Christians regarded the resurrection as an essential, and in some cases perhaps even the central, element of the Christian faith.

Why should the suggestion that Jesus was actually raised from the dead have become universally accepted among the first Christians? After two thousand years, Christians have got used to the idea of Jesus being raised from the dead. However, the idea is actually very strange. Even by the standards of the first century, it was an extraordinary belief. Far from merely fitting into the popular expectation of the pattern of resurrection, what happened to Jesus actually contradicted it. The sheer novelty of the Christian position at the time has been obscured by two thousand years' experience of the Christian understanding of the resurrection. At the time, however, it was wildly unorthodox and radical. To dismiss the Christian understanding of the resurrection of Jesus because it allegedly conformed to contemporary expectations is clearly unacceptable. Nobody was prepared for what happened.

Most Jews at this time seem to have believed in the resurrection of the dead. Yet the general belief of the time concerned the future resurrection of the dead, at the end of time itself. Nobody believed in a resurrection before the end of history. The Pharisees may be regarded as typical in this respect: they believed in a future resurrection, and held that men and women would be rewarded or punished after death, according to their actions. The Sadducees, however, insisted that there was no resurrection of any kind. No future existence awaited men and women after death. Paul was able to exploit the differences between the Pharisees and Sadducees on this point during an awkward moment in his career (see Acts 26:6–8).

The Christian claim thus does not fit any known Jewish pattern at all. The resurrection of Jesus is not declared to be a future event, but something which had already happened in the world of time and space, in front of witnesses. There was something quite distinct and unusual about the Christian claim that Jesus had been raised from the dead, which makes it rather difficult to account for. Why should the first Christians have believed something which was so strange by the standards of their time, unless something had happened which forced them to this conclusion – something unexpected and shattering, which called their existing ideas into question? The simplest answer is that they were confronted with the resurrection of Jesus, and had to rethink their entire world as a result.

It will thus be clear that the first Christians did not take on board a widespread Jewish belief, as some have suggested; they altered it dramatically. What the Jews thought could only happen at the end of the world was recognized to have happened in human history, before the end of time, and to have been seen and witnessed to by many. The totally unexpected event of the resurrection of Jesus, it would seem, caused the first Christians to break with the traditional belief concerning the resurrection.

The tomb of Jesus was empty
A second pointer to the resurrection is the tradition concerning the empty tomb. This is such a major element in each of the four gospels (Matthew 28:1–10; Mark 16:1–8; Luke 24:1–11; John 20:1–10) that it must be considered to have a basis in historical fact. The story is told from different aspects, and includes the divergence on minor points of detail which is so characteristic of eye-witness reports. Interestingly, all four gospels attribute the discovery of the empty tomb to women. The only Easter event to be explicitly related in detail by all four of the gospel writers is the visit of the women to the tomb of Jesus. Yet Judaism dismissed the value of the testimony or witness of women, regarding only men as having significant legal status in this respect. The greatest news that the world has ever known was first disclosed to women! Interestingly, Mark tells us the names of these women witnesses – Mary Magdalene, Mary the mother of James, and Salome – three times (Mark 15:40, 47; 16:1),

but never bothers to mention the names of any male disciples who were around at the time.

It is too easy for modern western readers, accustomed to a firm belief in the equality of men and women, to overlook the significance of this point. At the time, in the intensely patriarchal Jewish culture of that period, the testimony of a woman was virtually worthless. In first century Palestine, this would have been sufficient to discredit the accounts altogether. If the reports of the empty tomb were invented, it is difficult to understand why their inventors should have embellished their accounts of the 'discovery' with something virtually guaranteed to discredit them in the eyes of their audiences. Were the first Christians really that stupid? Why not attribute this discovery to men, if the story was just invented? The most obvious explanation is that the discoverers of the empty tomb were women, and that this was so well established within the early church that it could not be modified, even to make the story of the discovery of the empty tomb more plausible to male audiences.

Some have argued that the empty tomb is actually irrelevant, because it does not prove that the resurrection took place. It is difficult to follow the logic of this argument. It is certainly true that, taken by itself, the empty tomb does not prove that the resurrection took place. No Christian writer has suggested that the empty tomb, taken on its own, proves the resurrection of Jesus.

What we are talking about, however, is not a single piece of evidence, but the cumulative force of a number of pieces of evidence, which combine to give an essentially consistent picture of what happened on the first Easter Day, and its significance for believers. If the resurrection did indeed take place, one would expect the tomb to have been empty. It is therefore important to note the unanimous tradition of all four gospels to the effect that this was the case. It certainly does not prove that Christ was raised – but taken in conjunction with other pieces of evidence, it is seen to be of importance in establishing an overall picture of the event of the resurrection. The resurrection has many facets, of which the empty tomb is one. It proves nothing by itself. But it is not meant to be taken in isolation. Rather, it is to be seen as one aspect of a consistent overall picture of the resurrection.

One important additional consideration here is that the disciples were aware of the continuing presence of Jesus in their lives. There are persistent accounts in the New Testament documents of Jesus appearing to his disciples (such as Matthew 28:8–10, 16-20; Luke 24:13–43; John 20:11–29; Acts 1:1–11). Whatever we may make of these accounts, it is clear that the first Christians realized that the same person who had been crucified and buried was very much 'alive', in some sense of the word. Although he had unquestionably died, in some way – and the New Testament accounts of the resurrection appearances suggest that those who experienced Christ in this way found it difficult to put their experience into words – he still encountered men and women, and made himself known to them. Paul's references to this are of particular importance (1 Corinthians 15:3–8), in that Paul believed that it was the *risen* Christ who had appointed him as an apostle. We shall return to the importance of the resurrection for Paul later in this chapter.

The tomb of Jesus was not venerated by the disciples
A third key pointer to the resurrection is the lack of any form of tomb veneration amongst the disciples after the

death of Jesus. The practice of 'tomb veneration' – returning to the tomb of a prophet as a place of worship – was common in New Testament times. There is almost certainly a reference to it in Matthew 23:29–30. In fact, the tomb of David in Jerusalem is still venerated by many Jews to this day. But there is no record whatsoever of any such veneration of the tomb of Jesus by his disciples – an unthinkable omission, unless there was a very good reason for it. That reason appears to be the simple fact that Jesus' body was missing from its tomb. There seems to have been no dispute about this at the time. The rumour of Jesus' resurrection could have been put down without the slightest difficulty by the authorities simply by publicly displaying the corpse of Jesus.

It is of the greatest importance that the New Testament does not contain so much as the slightest trace of an attempt to reconcile belief in Jesus' resurrection with the existence of his corpse in some Palestinian grave. Nor is there any hint – in the New Testament, or anywhere else – that the Jewish or Roman authorities either produced, or attempted to produce, the corpse of Jesus. Had this been done, the preaching of the early church would have been discredited immediately. But the intriguing fact remains that no such move was made to discredit the first Christians' proclamation of the resurrection and its implications – and the simplest explanation of this remarkable omission is that the corpse was disquietingly absent from its tomb.

All the evidence indicates that the tomb was empty on the third day. The controversy at the time concerned not the *fact* of the empty tomb, but the *explanation* of that emptiness. Matthew records one explanation advanced by one group of critics of Jesus - the disciples had stolen the body at night (Matthew 28:12–15). But it is clear that the disciples believed in a somewhat more exciting explanation – that Jesus had been raised from the dead. Once more, we must emphasize this point: there can be no doubt that the first disciples did believe that Jesus had been raised by God. The reports concerning the empty tomb are completely consistent with this belief, and must be regarded as being at least as historically accurate as any report of any event from the time. Our task is simply to account for this belief, and ask whether it is likely to be correct.

The outlook of the disciples was transformed

A fourth factor to be taken into consideration is the transformation of the first Christians, and the remarkable advances which Christianity made in the period immediately after Christ's death. It is clear from the gospel accounts of Jesus' betrayal that the disciples were devastated by his arrest and execution. The fact that Peter was moved to deny Jesus at this point is particularly significant (Mark 14:66–72). The gospels do not record the presence of any of the leading disciples at Calvary. Mark notes the presence of three women in particular at the scene (Mark 15:40–41). However, his attention is mainly directed towards the reaction of the Roman centurion to Jesus' death (Mark 15:39); this important official publicly declared that Jesus was the Son of God. Mark also fails to note the presence of the disciples at Christ's burial (Mark 15:42–47), and goes to some lengths to emphasize that the only witnesses to Jesus' death and burial (Mary Magdalene and Mary the mother of James) were also those who first discovered the empty tomb (Mark 15:40, 47; 16:1–8). John's gospel notes that the disciples met secretly indoors in the aftermath of the crucifixion, 'for fear of the Jews' (John 20:19).

93

It is obvious from the gospel accounts of the crucifixion of Jesus that the first disciples thought that this was the end of everything. The man for whom they had given up everything to follow had been executed, without any sign of divine intervention. We can feel a profound sense of sadness as we read those gospel accounts. The disciples slink away, demoralized and dispirited. They give every impression of being hopeless and helpless, like sheep without a shepherd.

Suddenly, all this changes. This band of sad, demoralized cowards is transformed into a joyful group of potential martyrs, for whom death no longer holds any terror. Something totally unexpected has obviously happened. How else can we account for this remarkable transformation? A mass delusion, perhaps? Hypnosis? The alternatives are certainly there but they lack any real plausibility. As Pinchas Lapide, a leading Jewish scholar has perceptively remarked in his work *The Resurrection of Jesus*, 'Without the resurrection of Jesus, after Golgotha, there would not have been any Christianity'. This Jewish writer comments thus on the changed mood of the disciples:

> When this scared, frightened band of the apostles which was just about to throw away everything in order to flee in despair to Galilee; when these peasants, shepherds and fishermen, who betrayed and denied their master and then failed him miserably, suddenly could be changed into a confident mission society, convinced of salvation and able to work with much more success after Easter than before Easter, then no vision or hallucination is sufficient to explain such a revolutionary transformation.

This was no mistake, misapprehension or confusion. This was a realization that Jesus had been raised from the dead, as a new era in history dawned before their eyes.

If the accounts of the early church recorded in Acts are anything to go by, the disciples were transformed. An early Christian sermon recorded in Acts makes clear what brought about this remarkable change:

> This man [Jesus] was handed over to you by God's set purpose and foreknowledge; and you, with the help of wicked men, put him to death by nailing him to the cross. But God raised him from the dead, freeing him from the agony of death, because it was impossible for death to keep its hold on him. (Acts 2:23–24).

Note the emphasis upon the necessity of the crucifixion. The possibility that it was an accidental end to Jesus' ministry is excluded in favour of the view that this seemingly appalling and senseless event was part of God's intention for Jesus, possessing a deeper meaning and significance.

It is possible that the disciples were deluded idiots, who were content to be martyred for a myth. Many early Christians were subjected to persecution and various other forms of unpleasantness, and some executed, for reasons directly arising from their faith. The Book of Revelation, the final (and most enigmatic!) work in the New Testament, appears to have been written with this in mind. A similar situation may underlie the first letter of Peter. In both cases, a direct appeal is made to the resurrection of Jesus as a ground for hope in the face of such opposition, even when death is seen as the inevitable consequence.

Later, the practical results of martyrdom came to be more fully appreciated. The African Christian theologian Tertullian, writing in the early third century, remarked that 'the blood of the martyrs is the seed of the church'. In other words, martyrdom has useful propaganda value. But the early Christians appear to have been content to accept this fate on the basis of another consideration: the belief that those who suffered with Christ would one day be raised from the dead, just as he had been. They may have been completely deluded in this confident expectation, but there is no doubt that they firmly believed in it, and thus force us to account for the origins of the belief. As a piece of circumstantial evidence, it unquestionably points to something or other which gave rise to this belief, and the resurrection of Jesus is totally consistent with it.

The Acts of the Apostles also records a remarkable growth in the church at this early stage, a growth which continued in the period after that of the New Testament. Early Christianity was not spread at the point of the sword, by force, but through the persuasiveness of its preaching (and Acts may well give us insights into the nature of that preaching). By the early fourth century, Christianity had become so widespread and influential that it was recognized as the official religion of the Roman empire. From this point onwards, its successes must be put down as being at least in part due to its new official status. But before this point, it had nothing to commend it, except its beliefs. Of these beliefs, we know that the idea of resurrection was considered essential, and appears to have been a leading feature of early Christian preaching.

Despite hostility on every side, early Christianity possessed a vitality which kept it going and growing.

This vitality was unquestionably a reflection of a firm belief in the resurrection of Jesus. Once more, it is necessary to note the possibility that the early Christians were wrong in this belief (although some of the alternative explanations of the origins of this belief are more improbable than the idea of resurrection itself). But the fact still remains that this idea was central to the worship and preaching of the first Christians, as it remains so to this day.

Jesus is worshipped as the living and risen Lord
A fifth pointer to the resurrection lies in the remarkably exalted understandings of Jesus which became widespread within Christian circles so soon after his death. Jesus was not venerated as a dead prophet or rabbi, as we have already seen: he was worshipped as the living and risen Lord. The use of the word 'Lord' in the New Testament is worth noting, and we shall discuss it in the next chapter. At some places in the New Testament, Jesus appears to be explicitly identified with God himself, and some sort of implicit identification along these lines is widespread, and would become normative in the following centuries.

At several points in the New Testament, words originally referring to God himself are applied to Jesus. Two examples are especially interesting. In Romans 10:13, Paul states that 'everyone who calls upon the name of the Lord [Jesus, in this case] will be saved' – yet the original of this Old Testament quotation (Joel 2:32) is actually a statement to the effect that everyone who calls upon the name of God will be saved. In Philippians 2:10, Paul alters an Old Testament prophecy to the effect that everyone will one day bow at the name of God (Isaiah 45.23) to refer to Jesus.

Paul regarded this identification of Jesus and God as perfectly legitimate, on the basis of the resurrection. John's gospel bears witness to the crucial practice of referring to Jesus as 'Lord and God' (John 20:28) – a title which Thomas gave to Jesus, according to John, after being convinced that the resurrection really did take place. Thus Gregory Nazianzen, writing in the fourth century, stated that Christians believed in a 'God who was made flesh and put to death in order that we might live again'. The term *Theotokos* ('Bearer of God', or perhaps 'Mother of God') came to be used to refer to Mary in the fourth century, and was basically an expression of the belief that her child was (in some sense) none other than God himself.

How could this remarkable transformation in the perceived status of Jesus have come about? He died as a common criminal, perhaps a prophet, or maybe a martyr; but the most this would merit would be veneration of his tomb (see Matthew 23:29). Of course, we have already noted that there was a problem about Jesus' tomb, which was found to be empty so soon after his death. But the point still remains important: why did the early Christians start talking about a dead rabbi as if he were God? Perhaps even more interesting, why did they talk about him as if he was alive, praying to him, and worshipping him? Once more, we must note that it is possible that they were the victims of a hysterical delusion which has continued to this day. But another explanation is that they believed that Jesus had been raised from the dead by God, thus establishing or demonstrating the unique relationship between God and Jesus. It was on this unique relationship that the early Christians based their views of Jesus.

Christian worship points to the resurrection

Sixth, we must consider the way in which the first Christians worshipped in public. We know that two sacraments or rites became normative within the church in a remarkably short period, both being witnessed to in the New Testament itself. These are baptism and the rite now known variously as the 'Lord's Supper', 'breaking of bread', 'communion', or 'eucharist'. Both reflect a strong belief in the resurrection.

Paul states that baptism calls to mind the death and resurrection of Jesus (Romans 6:4–5). It is interesting that the early church baptized its converts on Easter Day, to bring home fully the significance of the resurrection to the sacrament. Equally, a strong belief in the resurrection has always led to the eucharist being seen as a celebration of the living presence of Christ in his church, rather than a veneration of a dead teacher. Baptism and eucharist alike are essentially celebrations of Christ's Easter victory, rather than solemn memorials of the debacle of Good Friday. The belief that the Jesus who was crucified is now alive and present within his church has exercised an enormous influence over Christian worship down the ages, going back to the earliest of times.

Christian experience points to the resurrection

Seventh, we must consider the Christian experience of Jesus down the ages. This is difficult to assess, because it is so subjective. However, it is clear that Christians experience Jesus in such a way that they cannot speak of him other than as a living Saviour and Lord. Jesus does not come to us as a dead teacher or past historical figure, but as a present and living reality. Paul's encounter with the risen Christ on the road to Damascus (described in Acts 9:1–9; 22:4–16; 26:9–18, and referred to in 1 Corinthians 15:8–9 and Galatians 1:11–24) has been paralleled in the Christian experience down the centuries to the present day. Whatever we may make of this fact, the point simply is this: Christians find it easy to believe in the resurrection of Jesus, basically because they feel they know or experience him here and now. This evidence would not stand up for one moment in a court of law, but it reminds us that Christianity is grounded in experience, and that the Christian experience of Jesus is consistent with the idea of his resurrection.

Objections to the resurrection

In the last chapter, we suggested that the gospels were rather like crime fiction, setting out clues as to what was going on. In her famous detective novel *The Unpleasantness at the Bellona Club*, set in London's high society during the 1920s, Dorothy L. Sayers opens the chapter describing Lord Peter Wimsey's breakthrough in the mystery surrounding the death of General Fentiman with the following words:

> 'What put you on to this poison business,' [Detective Inspector Parker] asked.
> 'Aristotle, chiefly,' replied Wimsey. 'He says, you know, that one should always prefer the probable impossible to the improbable possible. It was possible, of course, that the General should have died off in that neat way at the most confusing moment. But how much nicer and more probable that the whole thing had been stage-managed.'

Inevitably, we are faced with a similar dilemma in dealing with the resurrection of Jesus. There are a number of perfectly possible explanations of the evidence we noted above. Jesus may possibly have done nothing other than fainted on the cross, and revived in the tomb, to wander off into the unknown; the first Christians may possibly have been the victims of hysterical delusions; the 'resurrection' may possibly have been an invention of the disciples to cover up their own theft of Jesus' corpse from the tomb. These are all possibilities – but somehow, they seem terribly implausible, and do not stand up to critical scrutiny. They simply don't have the 'ring of truth' about them. They are 'improbable possibles', to use Wimsey's terms. And so we begin to consider the 'probable impossible' – that Jesus really did rise from the dead, and that this more than adequately accounts for the evidence in our possession. So important is this question that some would like further discussion of its central themes. So let us consider an 'improbable possible' – that Jesus simply fainted on the cross, so that the resurrection is a mistake of the highest order.

Jesus did not die: he just fainted

One theory is that Jesus did not really die on the cross, but fainted or swooned. His subsequent revival was then interpreted by some highly credulous disciples as a resurrection. But there is something very implausible about this. Is it really likely that experienced Roman executioners would have bungled Jesus' execution, knowing how important he was? Would such experienced executioners have been likely to confuse fainting and dying? Some nineteenth century rationalists certainly thought so, and their ideas have even found their way into more recent discussions of the subject.

The German writer H. E. G. Paulus put forward the following suggestion in 1828. In first century Palestine, it

101

was quite common for people to be buried when they weren't actually dead. This is what happened in the case of Jesus. He fainted on the cross. Now it is true, as Paulus concedes, that Jesus was stabbed with a spear before he was taken down from the cross (see John 19:34). But Paulus is thoroughly up to date with the latest medical theory (in 1828 that is). According to these reports, he argues, one way to make someone recover is to bleed them. So what really happened in the case of Jesus was that the spear did not actually penetrate Jesus' heart. It simply cut a vein, with a resulting loss of blood. The latest discoveries have shown that this would have helped Jesus recover from his trance.

Jesus' body was then taken to a grave. The smell of the spices in which he was wrapped, and the coolness of the tomb, combined to revive him, with the result that on the Sunday morning, he was able to leave the tomb. Fortunately, the great stone which had blocked the entrance had been moved by an earthquake, so he was able to get out without too much difficulty. Nearby he managed to find a set of gardener's clothes, which he put on (and, of course, Mary then mistook him for a gardener: John 20:15).

After that, Jesus put in the occasional appearance to his disciples, who, being unsophisticated and backward peasants, thought that he was risen from the dead. After forty days, however, he realized that he was finally going to die from his wounds, so climbed a nearby mountain to say goodbye to his followers. A cloud then appeared from somewhere, so that Jesus disappeared from view, going off somewhere (nobody knows where) never to be heard of again, and died.

Without wishing to seem disrespectful, this seems very difficult to take seriously. The possibility that a group of professional Roman executioners should have failed in their task is improbable enough. The reference to 'blood and water' when Jesus' side was pierced after the crucifixion (John 19:34) would seem to be a reference to separation of the blood into clot and serum, indicating that Jesus was unequivocally dead. As this presumably was not a known medical fact when John's gospel was written, it is unlikely to have been included to make the account seem more plausible. We are also asked to believe that this hungry, thirsty and seriously wounded man would have been able to unwind his grave-clothes and crawl from his tomb. Not only that, but we are asked to believe that he would have given his disciples the impression that he was the conqueror over death, when in fact he was obviously a seriously ill man who would die of his wounds shortly afterwards!

Now it is possible that someone who is deliberately determined not to believe in the resurrection may find this a convincing explanation. Some, prepared to clutch at any straw in order to avoid conceding the attraction and appeal of the gospel, argue that it is a perfectly respectable explanation of events. But most regard it with contempt. Even many critics of Christianity, however, find it totally implausible, saying little for the intelligence of those who suggest it. It is just not an adequate explanation. It rests on totally spurious foundations. The 'medical' evidence brought forward may have convinced Paulus (who was not, as need hardly be added, a physician himself, or even competent in the field); it failed to convince his readers.

But resurrections don't happen . . .
An objection may well be raised that the resurrection is simply an impossibility, and therefore cannot have

103

happened, no matter what the evidence may be suggesting that it did. This point is important, and we shall illustrate its fundamental weakness by looking at the famous debate between two German scholars over precisely this point.

Ernst Troeltsch, writing at the turn of the present century, argued that what he called the 'principle of analogy' must govern our thinking about Jesus. In other words, we should ask whether present-day analogies (that is, equivalent events) exist in the case of the events reported in the gospels. If they do exist, we may conclude that a reasonable foundation has been laid for establishing that these events actually did take place. Obviously, it does not prove that they did take place.

To give an example: Jesus was executed by crucifixion. There were countless analogies of the process of crucifixion as a form of execution at the time, for which we have excellent archaeological and literary evidence. The idea of 'execution' still has present-day analogies, although not in the more civilized parts of western Europe. We may therefore conclude that there is a real possibility that Jesus was executed by crucifixion. Now we must establish whether this possibility did, in fact, take place – and on the basis of the evidence available from the gospels, we may conclude with reasonable certainty that it did.

But what if an event recorded in the gospels, such as the resurrection of Jesus, is without a present-day analogy? This is claimed to be a unique event. No-one has ever been raised from the dead before (despite the occasional insignificant references to something possibly along the same lines in Egyptian or Nordic mythology). No-one presently alive has ever witnessed a resurrection; the Christian claim that Christ's resurrection is unique suggests that this is impossible anyway. Therefore, Troeltsch argued, we must conclude that the resurrection probably did not happen.

In response, let us suppose that something absolutely unique, which has never been repeated, took place about two thousand years ago, in an obscure part of the civilized world. (Perhaps a bloody corpse, fresh from an expert execution, and obviously dead, came back to life?) Accounts of it, ultimately going back to eyewitnesses, were written down shortly afterwards, and preserved to the present day. Would a present-day observer be inclined to believe that the event has actually happened? Probably not, unconsciously allowing his or her methods of investigation to dictate what could and could not have happened. There are excellent reasons for thinking that on the basis of the methods and presuppositions of some contemporary historians, unique and extraordinary events simply cannot be thought of as ever happening. So what happens if one actually did take place?

Although Troeltsch's point was taken seriously by scholars for several decades, it is now regarded as somewhat old-fashioned. The most important criticism of it to have been made recently is due to the brilliant and greatly respected German theologian Wolfhart Pannenberg. Pannenberg criticized this approach along the following lines. The 'principle of analogy' is basically a useful tool for historical research. Troeltsch, however, has turned it into a dogmatic view of reality. In other words, because we have no present-day analogies of something, it simply cannot have happened in the first place. A unique event is therefore excluded from the outset, because it does not have any parallels today. The resurrection thus cannot have happened, because dead people do not rise from the dead. In other words, resurrections do not happen, so the resurrection of Jesus cannot have happened.

But, as Pannenberg emphasizes, all that Troeltsch is doing is to exclude the resurrection as a matter of principle, no matter what the evidence in favour of it may be. This, he argues, is lousy history. According to Pannenberg, we should abandon this unjustified dogmatic view of what can and cannot happen, and simply concentrate on the evidence for the resurrection with open minds about its possibility. According to Pannenberg, the evidence in favour of the resurrection being a real historical event is decisive. Like Lord Peter Wimsey in Dorothy Sayer's tale, we must abandon our preconceived ideas about what can happen and what cannot, and be open-minded about the evidence.

One final point needs to be made here. The resurrection of Jesus is closely linked with his divinity. Troeltsch's argument actually takes the following form: no mere human being has ever been raised from the dead in recent experience. Therefore, no mere human could have been raised from the dead in the past. But, as we have seen, Jesus does not belong to this category. He is no mere human, but is God incarnate. Jesus stands outside the category which Troeltsch excludes from being raised from the dead. That sets his argument in a rather different perspective.

The meaning of the resurrection

Christ was raised from the dead. So what? What is the relevance of this event? What is the *meaning* of the resurrection? The New Testament gives us several answers to this question. It shows us how the resurrection was good news personally to certain individuals in particular and to believers in general, and explores the

ficance of the resurrection for the identity of Jesus.
egin by looking at the more personal aspects of the
.rrection, before considering its second aspect in the
ollowing chapter.

The resurrection transformed the lives of individuals.
John 20:11–18 is an account of how the resurrection was
recognized to be good news by Mary Magdalene, a
grieving and distraught individual, convinced that she
has lost her Lord for ever: 'They have taken my Lord
away, and I don't know where they have put him' (John
20:13). The moment of recognition, in which Mary suddenly realizes who it is who is addressing her, is often
regarded as one of the more tender moments of the New
Testament. The moment of recognition, and the simulta-
neous dawning of hope and joy, are a powerful testimony to the personal relevance of the gospel of the
resurrection in this case.

In Peter we encounter a betrayer, a failed apostle
who denied Christ when he was convinced he would
have given his life for the privilege of confessing his
name. Peter was called to be an apostle by the lakeside
(Luke 5:1–11). The scene of his failure was the charcoal
fire in the courtyard of the High Priest (John 18:18). With
great skill, John draws our attention to the fact that the
final encounter between Peter and the disciples and the
risen Lord incorporates both these elements in a new
commissioning by the risen Christ (John 21:1–19). The
symbols of calling and failure are there, reminding them
of the past; the risen Christ is also there, the symbol of
hope, forgiveness and a new beginning, summed up in
the new commissioning of the disciples. Peter will not
fail to confess Christ again. In an aside, we are reminded
of the price he would finally pay for that confession
(John 21:19).

The resurrection is also good news for believers today. It brings us hope, by assuring us that we shall share in the resurrection of Jesus, and be with him for ever. Nothing, not even death, can break the bonds which unite us to him. To become a Christian is to begin a relationship with Jesus Christ as our living Lord and Saviour which is not ended by death, but is rather brought to its consummation. We need not bid farewell to Jesus when we die; we can rest assured that we will be raised with him for ever. The resurrection also reminds us that there are no doors which are closed to the healing presence of Jesus. Suffering and death are both shown to have been conquered by him, a theme to which we shall return later.

The theme of hope is of central importance in human history. Despair drives peoples and societies into all kinds of disasters. A faith which offers the world no hope is irrelevant; a faith which offers the world a false hope is fraudulent. One of the greatest wonders of the gospel is that it offers the world a real hope, grounded in the bedrock of history, and guaranteed by the presence and power of the risen Lord Jesus. Jesus chose to suffer and die, so that those who put their trust in him might suffer and die in hope.

Since the New Testament, Christians have used the bread and wine of the Communion service in public worship as a reminder of the hope which the death and resurrection of Christ brings to his people. The bread and wine are symbols of suffering and death, transformed to joy and hope. An illustration may help to bring out the importance of this point.

The full impact of the horror of the First World War upon the British people can never be fully appreciated by those who did not go through it themselves. (It is

108

captured, to some extent, in Dorothy L. Sayer's novel *The Unpleasantness at the Bellona Club*, mentioned earlier, which is set in the period immediately following the First World War.) The most appalling carnage and suffering was seen on the battlefields of Flanders, on the banks of the Somme, and elsewhere. As people looked back on this war, it was hoped that it would be the war to end all wars, and that the death and suffering of so many might not be in vain. A symbol was chosen to express this hope of peace arising from the carnage of war: the poppy. In the blood-drenched ground of Flanders, beautiful red poppies sprang up, and were seen as symbols of hope, of new life in the face of death. So the poppy was worn on the anniversary of the ending of the First World War, to remind all of the carnage of war, and the hope that sprang up in its aftermath. All too soon, of course, it became clear that this was probably a vain hope.

In many ways, the bread and wine of the eucharist symbolize something very similar to those poppies: life through death, hope in the face of apparent despair. The bread and wine are the poppies of the cross, symbolizing the Christian hope of eternal life in the midst of a world of death and decay, established on the basis of the crucifixion and resurrection of Christ. It is this element of hope – in the Christian sense of a sure and confident expectation that God will raise us up as he once raised Christ – that underlies the Christian celebration and proclamation of Christ's death and resurrection through the Lord's Supper. In the words of the English poet George Herbert (1593–1633):

> Rise, heart, thy Lord is risen. Sing his praise
> Without delays,

Who takes thee by the hand, that thou likewise
With him mayst rise.

The resurrection means that the limitations of space and time are abolished. We do not need to be born again as first century Palestinians to encounter Christ, for the risen Christ finds us and calls us, whatever our situation. He breaks down historical and cultural barriers, and ultimately the barrier of death itself, precisely because he is risen and alive. For human beings, death means a severing of relationships, in that we are cut off from those whom we know and love. In the case of Jesus, we find that his death had exactly the opposite effect: on account of the resurrection, it restored him to fellowship with those whom he loved (Mary Magdalene being a good example) and opened up the possibility of fellowship with those whom (so to speak) he had never known – like us.

I once listened to a recording of some speeches made by the British prime minister, Winston Churchill, during the Second World War, at a time when Britain seemed to be about to be invaded and overwhelmed by Nazi armies. As I listened to these speeches, I became conscious of how Churchill had a remarkable grasp of rhetoric, a way of using words to great effect, denied to lesser mortals like myself. However, despite the splendour of his rhetoric, it was clear that he was a voice from the past, speaking about events in the past. I was listening to him out of curiosity, not because what he was saying had the slightest relevance to my own situation. The Second World War was long since over, something to be read about in history books, rather than a crucial struggle under way at this very moment, with its outcome uncertain. There was no longer any danger of being surrounded by Nazi troops.

The contrast with Jesus could not be more obvious. Christians simply cannot think of Jesus in terms of a revered former leader, who is now dead and gone. Nor is he someone who we merely read about in history textbooks. He is experienced as a present reality through being raised from the dead. Jesus is a living presence among his people, not a distant echo from the past. Moreover, the human situation remains much as it has ever been. We continue to be frail and sinful people, who need hope and joy in the face of death and despair. As long as men and women walk the face of this earth, knowing that they will die, the resurrection of Jesus Christ will continue to be good news to them.

Earlier, I pointed out that in Christ, the messenger and the message coincide. Christianity is about a relationship with a living person, not just believing certain ideas. All of us, especially those interested in the history of ideas, are only too painfully aware of the way in which intellectual fashions change. Philosophical ideas which were adopted by one generation are often just abandoned (rather than actually disproved) by another. The astonishingly rapid collapse of Hegelianism in Germany in the last century is a case in point. It is almost as if humanity wanders from one set of 'isms' to another, only to turn, dissatisfied, to yet another. Although Christianity can be stated (although not entirely satisfactorily) in terms of philosophical ideas of one sort or another, it is basically about the identity and significance of a *person* – a person who always takes precedence over the ideas through which his significance and relevance are expressed.

When addressing the Christians at Corinth (1 Corinthians 1:17 – 2:5), Paul emphasized that the gospel was not about human wisdom, but about the power of God demonstrated in the cross of Christ. Despite all the changes in the world of ideas that the last two thousand years have seen, the gospel has not become irrelevant in the way that so many philosophical systems – each of which was modern and relevant in its own day – have done. Why not? Because what is passed down from one generation to another is the experience of the presence of the crucified and risen Christ.

One generation may attempt to explain its significance in Hegelian terms, and another in existentialist terms – but the death of Hegelianism, for example, did not bring with it the death of Christianity. Each generation may (and, indeed, must) try to explain the identity and significance of Jesus in ideas or terms which make sense to its contemporaries – but what is passed on from one generation to another is not these abstract ideas or terms, but the living personal reality which lies behind them. To take the resurrection seriously is to realize that the living and risen Christ is, to put it crudely, much bigger than any one generation's apprehension or understanding of him, and that he will be equally really present to future generations, despite differences in culture or intellectual outlook.

We now turn to consider the New Testament understanding of the identity of Jesus. In what ways did the first Christians understand Jesus? Who did they think he was?

6

The New Testament witness to the person of Jesus

The New Testament presents us with a scintillating portrayal of the person of Jesus Christ. A vast assembly of material is brought together. The four gospels present us with information about his birth, life, death and resurrection, and document his remarkable impact upon those who he met. The Acts of the Apostles tells us of the experience of the risen Christ in the early church, and the rapid expansion of his influence through the thrilling preaching of those who had discovered him. The letters, especially those of Paul, present us with sustained reflection on the identity and significance of Jesus Christ for Christians and for the world.

The complexity of the New Testament witness
The witness of the New Testament to Jesus Christ is complex. At times, it explicitly refers to him as God; at others, it uses highly suggestive titles to refer to him – such as Messiah, Son of God, Lord, Saviour. We shall look at some of these titles, and attempt to make sense

of them, before looking at the most powerful and profound way of thinking about Jesus – the doctrine of the incarnation – in the chapters which follow.

•   Before we do this, however, we must remember that the New Testament witness to Jesus concerns far more than the titles it uses to refer to him. It focuses on the claims he made, the things he did, the impact he had on those who encountered him, the worship that was paid to him, and his resurrection from the dead. We are presented with a complex overall picture, and we cannot really isolate fragments of it, and declare that this or that idea embodies the totality of the New Testament witness to Jesus. A holistic approach is called for.

The most remarkable feature of the New Testament is not so much that it refers to Jesus as 'Saviour' or 'Lord', or that he was worshipped by the early Christians, or that he was raised from the dead, but that all these things, and many more besides, are true of the one and the same person. These may be seen as the development of perfectly legitimate insights into the identity and significance of Jesus, rather than as inventions or serious distortions of the evidence.

Christians are people who *think* about their faith. Part of that process of thinking through the significance of Jesus involves asking the following question: who must Jesus *be* if all these things are true about him? The facts about Jesus were such that it was appropriate and necessary to refer to him in the way that we actually find in the New Testament. There is every reason to suppose that there was a direct, continuous and unbroken line between the historical figure of Jesus of Nazareth and the church's Christological interpretation of his identity and significance. What caused the first Christians to speak about Jesus in these ways?

114

In part, the answer relates to a new experience of God, mediated through the risen Christ. The first Christians regarded Jesus as both the source and the object of their religious experience. Their experience of God was recognized as depending on him, and deriving from him. The conviction that Jesus was a present and living reality, the source of authentic experience of God, is deeply embedded in the New Testament. Jesus is not understood as an example of how we experience God, but as the source of our experience of God. He is the object of our experience of God, in that Jesus may be said to be experienced in the same way as God. The idea that Jesus can simply be described as a 'teacher' or 'moral example' is seriously deficient in this vital respect. We are not being asked simply to obey or imitate Christ, but are being invited to share by faith in the new way of life that has been made possible through his saving death and resurrection.

This brings out how appallingly inadequate it is to suggest that Jesus relates to Christians in much the same way as a rabbi relates to his disciples, or the founder of a university to his students (to use two reductionist analogies which were favourites with rationalist writers of the eighteenth century). It is tempting to suggest that those who speak of Jesus in this way have never really experienced the profound and vital impact of Christianity, perhaps overlooking (and certainly minimizing) the experiential aspects of faith in Christ. Certainly Jesus is revered and imitated, to the somewhat limited extent that is possible; however, the Christian experience of Jesus far transcends this. Once more, we must pause and reflect upon the impact and relevance of the resurrection upon the first Christians for a proper understanding of the crucified Jesus.

The gospels and their audiences

The complex New Testament witness to Jesus Christ is probably best understood as a gradual drawing out of something which was always there from the beginning. The first Christians were confronted with something so exciting and novel in the life, death and resurrection of Jesus that they were obliged to employ a whole range of images, terms and ideas to describe it. There was simply no single term available which could capture the richness and profundity of their impressions and experience of Jesus. They were forced to use a whole variety of terms to illuminate the different aspects of their understanding of him. Taken together, these combine to build up an overall picture of Christ.

At times they may even have drawn upon ideas or concepts ultimately deriving from paganism to try and build up this picture. For example, it is often thought that John 1:1–18, with its emphasis on the 'Word' (Greek: *Logos*), is trying to show that Jesus occupies the same place in the Christian understanding of the world as the idea of the *Logos* occupies in secular Greek philosophy. But this does not mean that Christians invented their understanding of Jesus' significance because they happened to read a few textbooks of Stoic philosophy. Rather, they noticed an analogy or parallel, and saw the obvious advantages to be gained by exploiting it to express something which they already knew about. It also went some way to make Christianity more understandable to an educated Greek audience. Even at this early stage in the Christian tradition, we can see a principled determination to make the gospel both intelligible and accessible to those outside the church. The gospel was thus expressed using ideas and concepts which helped to bring out its central themes, and make

116

them understandable to non-believers.

We know that the early Christian church exploded – there is really no other word which describes the impact which it made! – into the first century mediterranean world. In the course of this astonishingly rapid advance, it encountered both Jewish and Greek cultures. The Jews already knew all about ideas like 'Messiah' and 'Son of God', which made it easy for the Christians to explain their understanding of Jesus to them. It was thus only necessary to persuade them that Jesus was indeed the fulfilment of the great Old Testament prophecies, the long-promised Messiah. Matthew's gospel seems to have been written with this sort of audience in mind. In Chapter 4, we noticed how often he points out the parallels between Jesus' ministry and Old Testament prophecies. The phrase 'this took place to fulfil the prophecy of . . .' dominates the first few chapters of his gospel.

In the case of the Greeks, this was more difficult. After all, the Christians could hardly have expected their Greek audience to have read the entire Old Testament before they could have the gospel explained to them. They therefore used analogies and ideas which would express their understanding of the identity and significance of Jesus in terms that their Greek readers could understand . An excellent example of this is provided by Paul's 'Areopagus Sermon' (Acts 17:16–34). This sermon, preached to philosophers at the Areopagus (or 'Mars Hill') in Athens, aims to gain a hearing for the gospel by engaging with ideas and terms which were already familiar to Paul's audience.

Luke's gospel is another case in point. Luke is clearly writing for an audience which includes non-Jews (usually referred to as 'Gentiles'). The word 'Messiah' would have meant little to such a readership, who would not have been fully aware of its implications and nuances. However, many of the Greek religions were already used to terms such as 'Saviour' or 'Redeemer'. By using such terms, and always interpreting them in a rigorously Christian manner, Luke could express the significance of Jesus Christ in terms which would have made sense to his readers.

In doing this, Luke was in no way inventing the significance of Jesus, nor was he forcing Jesus into a pagan religious context. He was simply bringing out the full significance of Jesus, using words and ideas to which his readers could respond. In this way, Luke opened the way for a pagan readership to discover that the true fulfilment of their religious hopes lay only in Jesus Christ.

All that such Christian writers were doing was expressing something they already knew, something that was already there and already true, in new and different ways, in order to get their message across. The fact that Christianity found it so easy to cross cultural barriers at the time is a remarkable testimony to the effectiveness of the first Christians' attempts to express their beliefs in ways that made sense outside a Jewish context.

New Testament titles for Jesus

The issues just touched on are fascinating, and are worth exploring in considerably more detail, to bring out the depth and richness of the New Testament understanding of the person of Jesus Christ. But enough has been said to allow us to begin to explore four of the specific titles used by New Testament writers to refer to Jesus, and examine some of their implications for our understanding of the identity and significance of Jesus.

Messiah

We begin by considering the title 'the Christ', or 'the Messiah'. These two words refer to the same idea, the former being the Greek version, the latter the Hebrew. (Interestingly, both the Greek and Hebrew words are mentioned together in John 1:41). When Peter recognizes Jesus as 'the Christ, the Son of the living God' (Matthew 16:16), he is identifying Jesus with the long-awaited Messiah. It is very easy for a modern western reader to assume that 'Christ' was Jesus' surname, and to fail to appreciate that it is actually a title – 'Jesus the Christ'.

The term 'Messiah' literally means 'the anointed one' – someone who has been anointed with oil. This Old Testament practice indicated that the person anointed in this way was regarded as having been singled out by God as having special powers and functions; thus 1 Samuel 24:6 refers to the king as 'the Lord's anointed'. The basic sense of the word could be said to be 'the divinely appointed King of Israel'. As time passed, the term gradually came to refer to a deliverer, himself a descendent of David, who would restore Israel to the golden age she enjoyed under the rule of David.

During the period of Jesus' ministry, Palestine was occupied and administered by Rome. There was fierce nationalist feeling at the time, fuelled by intense resentment at the presence of a foreign occupying power, and this appears to have given a new force to the traditional expectation of the coming of the Messiah. For many, the Messiah would be the deliverer who expelled the Romans from Israel, and restored the line of David. Jesus refused to see himself as Messiah in this sense. At no point in his ministry do we find any violence against Rome suggested or condoned, nor even an explicit attack on the Roman administration. Jesus' attacks are directed primarily against his own people. Thus after his triumphal entry into Jerusalem (Matthew 21:8–11), which gives every indication of being a deliberate Messianic demonstration or gesture, Jesus immediately evicts the merchants from the temple (Matthew 21:12–13).

Interestingly, Jesus was not prepared to accept the title 'Messiah' in the course of his ministry. Mark's gospel should be read carefully to note this point. When Peter acclaims Jesus as Messiah – 'You are the Christ!' – Jesus immediately tells him to keep quiet about it (Mark 8:29–30). It is not clear what the full significance of the 'Messianic secret' is. Why should Mark emphasize that Jesus did not make an explicit claim to be the Messiah, when he was so clearly regarded as such by so many?

Perhaps the answer may be found later in Mark's gospel, when he recounts the only point at which Jesus explicitly acknowledges his identity as the Messiah. When Jesus is led, as a prisoner, before the High Priest, he admits to being the Messiah (Mark 14:61–62). Once violent or political action of any sort is no longer possible, Jesus reveals his identity. He was indeed the deliverer of the people of God – but not, it would seem, in any political sense of the term. The misunderstandings associated with the term, particularly in Zealot circles, appear to have caused Jesus to play down the Messianic side of his mission.

The Jews did not expect their Messiah to be executed as a common criminal. It is worth noting that, immediately after Peter acknowledges Jesus as the Messiah, Jesus begins to explain to his disciples that he must suffer, be rejected by his own people, and be killed (Mark 8:29–31) – hardly an auspicious end to a Messianic career. Paul made it clear to the Corinthian Christians that the very idea of 'a crucified Messiah' (or 'a crucified

Christ') was scandalous to a Jew (1 Corinthians 1:23). From a very early stage, it is clear that Christians recognized a link between Jesus' Messiahship and the destiny of the mysterious 'Suffering Servant':

> He was despised, and rejected . . . a man of sorrows, and familiar with suffering . . . he was despised, and we esteemed him not. Surely he took up our infirmities and carried our sorrows, yet we considered him stricken by God, smitten by him and afflicted. But he was pierced for our transgressions, he was crushed for our iniquities; the punishment that brought us peace was upon him, and by his wounds we are healed . . . the Lord has laid on him the iniquity of us all (Isaiah 53:3–6).

Lord

A second title which claims our attention is 'Lord' (Greek: *kyrios*). The word is used in two main senses in the New Testament. It is used as a polite title of respect, particularly when addressing someone. Thus when I write a letter to my bank manager, beginning 'Dear Sir,' I am not for one moment implying that he has been knighted; I am just being polite. So it is with several passages in the New Testament. When Martha speaks to Jesus, and addresses him as 'Lord' (John 11:21), she is probably, although not necessarily, merely treating Jesus with proper respect.

Of infinitely greater importance, however, are the frequent passages in the New Testament in which Jesus is referred to as 'the Lord'. The confession that 'Jesus is Lord' (Romans 10:9; 1 Corinthians 12:3) was clearly regarded by Paul as a statement of the essential feature of the gospel. Christians are those who 'call upon the name of the Lord' (Romans 10:13; 1 Corinthians 1:2). But what is implied by this? It is clear that there was a tendency in first century Palestinianism to use the word 'Lord' (Greek: *kyrios*; Aramaic: *mare*) to designate a divine being, or at the very least a figure who is decidedly more than just human, in addition to its function as a polite or honorific title. But of particular importance is the use of this Greek word *kyrios* to translate the cypher of four letters used to refer to God in the Old Testament (often referred to as the 'Tetragrammaton', from the Greek words for 'four' and 'letters').

The Old Testament writers were reluctant to refer to God directly, apparently regarding this as compromising his transcendence. On occasions where it was necessary to make reference to God, they tended to use a 'cypher' of four letters, sometimes transliterated into English as YHWH. This group of letters, which lies behind the King James Version references to God as 'Jehovah', and the Jerusalem Bible's references to God as 'Yahweh', was used to represent the sacred name of God. Other Hebrew words could be used to refer to gods in general; this name was used to refer only to the 'God of Abraham, Isaac and Jacob'. It is specific to God, almost acting as a proper name. It is never used to refer to any other divine or angelic being, unlike other Hebrew words for 'god'. These latter words act as common nouns, referring to 'god' or 'gods' in general, and can be used to refer to Israel's own God, or to other gods (such as the pagan gods of other nations). But the Tetragrammaton is used only to name the specific God which Israel knew and worshipped, and who is made known through the life, death and resurrection of Jesus Christ.

When the Old Testament was translated from

Hebrew into Greek, the word *kyrios* was generally used to translate the sacred name of God. Of the 6,823 times that this name is used in the Hebrew, the Greek word *kyrios* ('Lord') is used to translate it on 6,156 occasions. This Greek word thus came to be an accepted way of referring directly and specifically to the God who had revealed himself to Israel at Sinai, and who had entered into a covenant with his people on that occasion. Jews would not use this term to refer to anyone or anything else. To do so would be to imply that this person or thing was of divine status. The historian Josephus tells us that the Jews refused to call the Roman Emperor *kyrios*, because they regarded this name as reserved for God alone.

The writers of the New Testament had no hesitation in using this sacred name to refer to Jesus, with all that this implied. A name which was used exclusively to refer to God was regarded as referring equally to Jesus. This was not some error made by ill-informed writers, ignorant of the Jewish background to the name. After all, the first disciples were Jews. Those New Testament writers, such as Paul, who make most use of the term 'Lord' to refer to Jesus were perfectly well aware of its implications. Yet they regarded the evidence concerning Jesus, especially his resurrection from the dead, as compelling them to make this statement concerning his identity. It was a deliberate, considered, informed and justified decision, which is entirely appropriate in the light of the history of Jesus. He has been raised to glory and majesty, and sits at the right hand of God. He therefore shares the same status as God and is to be addressed accordingly.

On occasion, the New Testament takes an Old Testament reference to 'the Lord' (in other words, 'the Lord

God'), and deliberately applies or transfers this to 'the Lord Jesus'. Perhaps the most striking example of this tendency may be seen by comparing Joel 2:32 with Acts 2:21. The passage in Joel refers to a coming period in the history of the people of God, in which the Spirit of God will be poured out upon all people (Joel 2:28). On this 'great and dreadful day of the Lord' (that is, God) 'everyone who calls upon the name of the Lord will be saved' (Joel 2:31–32) – in other words, all who call upon the name of *God* will be saved.

This prophecy is alluded to in Peter's great sermon on the Day of Pentecost (Acts 2:17–21), which ends with the declaration that 'everyone who calls upon the name of the Lord shall be saved' (Acts 2:21). It is then made clear, in what follows, that the 'Lord' in question is none other than 'Jesus of Nazareth', whom God has made 'both Lord and Christ' (Acts 2:36). Peter declares that the resurrection has established that the same Jesus who was crucified has now been publicly declared by God to be the Messiah and Lord, with the right to equal status with God.

A further interesting example may be found in the use made of Isaiah 45:23 in Philippians 2:10–11. Isaiah speaks prophetically of a day in which 'the Lord' (that is, 'the Lord God') declares that 'every knee shall bow' to him, and 'every tongue confess him'. It is a powerful passage, in which the uniqueness of the God of Israel, and especially his universal claims to authority and sovereignty, are firmly stated (Isaiah 45:22–25). Paul identifies 'the Lord' as Jesus in the following passage:

> Therefore God exalted him to the highest place
> and gave him the name that is above every
> name, that at the name of Jesus every knee

> should bow . . . and every tongue confess that
> Jesus Christ is Lord, to the glory of God the
> Father (Philippians 2:9–11).

It is the lordship of Jesus Christ, publicly demonstrated
through the resurrection, which is to be acknowledged
by all. A further example is found in Hebrews 1:10,
which transfers the reference of Psalm 102:25 from God
to Jesus. Both Peter and Paul were Jews, who knew that
there was only one Lord and only one God. Only the
most persuasive of evidence could have forced them to
begin speaking of Jesus as God. Yet the resurrection and
exaltation of Jesus left them with no options. Here was
none other than God himself.

This practice of transferring from one Lord ('the
Lord God') to another ('the Lord Jesus') is known to
have infuriated Jews at the time. In the second-century
dialogue between Trypho the Jew and Justin Martyr,
Trypho complains that Christians have 'hijacked' passages referring to God, in order to refer them to Christ.
There was, of course, no suggestion that there were two
'Lords' (in other words, two Gods), simply that Jesus had
to be regarded as having a status at least equal to that of
God, which demanded that he be addressed and worshipped as such. The use of the term 'Lord' to refer to
Jesus may therefore be seen as a recognition of his
exalted status, arising from his resurrection.

Son of God
A further title used by the New Testament to refer to
Jesus is 'Son of God'. In the Old Testament, the term is
occasionally used to refer to angelic or supernatural
persons (see Job 38:7; Daniel 3:25). Messianic texts in the
Old Testament refer to the coming Messiah as the 'Son

of God' (2 Samuel 7:12–14; Psalm 2:7). The New Testament use of the term seems to mark a development of its Old Testament meaning, with an increased emphasis upon its exclusiveness.

Although all people are children of God in some sense of the word, Jesus is *the* Son of God. Paul distinguishes between Jesus as the natural Son of God, and believers as adopted sons. Their relation to God is quite different from Jesus' relationship to him, even though both may be referred to as 'sons of God'. We shall explore this point further when we consider the idea of 'adoption' as a way of thinking about the benefits which Christ obtained for us on the cross. Similarly, in the first letter of John, Jesus is referred to as 'the Son', while believers are designated as 'children'. There is something quite distinct about Jesus' relation to God, as expressed in the title 'Son of God'.

The New Testament understanding of Jesus' relationship to God, expressed in the Father–Son relationship, takes a number of forms. First, we note that Jesus directly addresses God as 'Father', with the very intimate Aramaic word 'Abba' being used (Mark 14:36: see also Matthew 6:9; 11:25–26; 26:42; Luke 23:34, 46). Secondly, it is clear from a number of passages that the evangelists regard Jesus as the Son of God, or that Jesus treats God as his father, even if this is not stated explicitly (Mark 1:11; 9:7; 12:6; 13:32; 14:61–62; 15:39). Thirdly, John's gospel is permeated with the Father–Son relationship (note especially passages such as John 5:16–27; 17:1–26), with a remarkable emphasis upon the identity of will and purpose of the Father and Son, indicating how close the relationship between Jesus and God was understood to be by the first Christians. At every level in the New Testament – in the words of Jesus himself, or in the impression which was created among the first Christians – Jesus is clearly understood to have a unique and intimate relationship to God, which the resurrection demonstrated publicly (Romans 1:3–4).

God

Finally, we need to consider a group of New Testament texts which make the most important and exciting assertion of all: that Jesus is none other than God. All the other material we have considered in this chapter can be seen as pointing to this conclusion. The affirmation that Jesus is divine is the climax of the New Testament witness to the person of Jesus Christ. At least ten texts in the New Testament seem to speak explicitly of Jesus in this way (John 1:1; 1:18; 20:28; Romans 9:5; Titus 2:13; Hebrews 1:8–9; 2 Peter 1:1 and 1 John 5:20). Others point in this direction, implying the same conclusion (such as Matthew 1:23; John 17:3; Galatians 2:20; Ephesians 5:5; Colossians 2:2; 2 Thessalonians 1:12 and 1 Timothy 3:16). We shall consider some of these verses in what follows.

One of the most remarkable passages in the New Testament describes how the doubts of Thomas concerning the resurrection of Jesus are dispelled (John 20:24–29). Thomas doubted that Jesus really had been raised. However, those doubts give way to faith when the risen Jesus is able to show him the wounds inflicted upon him at the crucifixion. Thomas responds with a declaration of faith in Christ, addressing him with the following words: 'My Lord and my God!' (John 20:28). These remarkable words are totally consistent with the witness to the identity of Jesus Christ which is provided by this gospel. We have already noted how the term 'Lord' could be used as a way of referring to God. However, Thomas explicitly addresses Jesus, not merely as

'Lord' but as 'God', making explicit what might otherwise only be implicit.

One of the great climaxes of Mark's gospel is reached towards its conclusion when a centurion, watching Christ die on the cross, declares 'surely this man was the Son of God' (Mark 15:39). These words of an eyewitness to the crucifixion can be seen as endorsing all that Mark wants us to know about the identity of Jesus. In a similar way, the words of Thomas, a witness to the reality of the resurrection of Jesus, allow John to bring his gospel to a superb climax.

The second letter of Peter is one of the later writings in the New Testament. It opens with a ringing declaration concerning the identity of Jesus Christ. The letter is addressed to 'those who through the righteousness of our God and Saviour Jesus Christ have received a faith as precious as ours' (2 Peter 1:1). A similar phrase is found in Paul's letter to Titus, which refers to Jesus Christ as 'God our Saviour' (Titus 1:3). The Greek form of both these statements makes it clear that they cannot be translated as if 'God' and 'Saviour' were different persons. Both titles clearly refer to the one and same person, Jesus Christ.

We could continue this examination of the various titles which the New Testament employs to refer to Jesus, to illustrate the many facets of its complex witness to his identity and significance. There is, however, a danger that by doing this, we may miss seeing the wood for the trees. In other words, we will fail to see that these titles, together with the New Testament accounts of the impact Christ had upon those whom he encountered, build up to give a pattern. The New Testament bears witness to Jesus as the embodiment of all God's promises, witnessed to in the Old Testament, brought to fulfilment and fruition.

The statements made about Jesus may be broadly listed under two classes. First, we have statements about Jesus' *function* – what God has done for us in Jesus. Secondly, we have statements about Jesus' *identity* – who he is. The two are, of course, closely connected. His achievements are grounded in his identity; his identity is demonstrated in his achievements. As the pieces of a jigsaw puzzle build up to give a pattern, which no single piece can show on its own, so the New Testament 'Christological titles' build up to give an overall picture, which no single title can adequately disclose. Taken collectively, they build up into a rich, deep and powerfully persuasive portrait of Christ as the divine Saviour and Lord, who continues to exercise an enormous influence over, and appeal to, sinful and mortal human beings.

7

Jesus as God: the doctrine

Jesus was human. Of that, the New Testament leaves us in no doubt. He was thirsty; he was tired; he suffered; he died. It also leaves us in no doubt that he was more than a man. The question is: in what sense was Jesus more than just a man? The full Christian answer to this question is complex, and will be explored in the remainder of this book. However, it will be helpful to anticipate the outline of that answer at this early stage.

Christianity declares that the only way of doing full justice to Jesus Christ is to recognize that he is both God and a man. Jesus is both divine and human. This central Christian doctrine is sometimes referred to as the 'doctrine of the two natures of Christ' (or sometimes just the 'doctrine of the two natures'). It can also be stated in the form of 'the doctrine of the incarnation', which focuses on the fact that God chose to enter into our world in Jesus Christ. (The word 'incarnation' comes from the Latin, and means 'being in the flesh'.) This theme of God entering into our world in Christ is set out clearly in the opening section of John's gospel (John 1:1–18), which culminates in the statement that 'The Word became flesh and made his dwelling among us. We have seen his glory, the glory of the One and Only, who came from the Father, full of grace and truth ' (John 1:14).

So important is this statement that it merits further analysis. The *Word* (the term used for one who is living, imperishable, creative and divine) *became* (entered into human history) *flesh* (the term used for what is creaturely, perishable, finite, mortal and human). The idea of 'incarnation' simply means God taking on human flesh, humbling himself to enter into human history and take on himself the entire experience of existence as a human being. He who was there from the beginning, the one who was God, became a human being, in order to redeem us. As the famous Christmas carol *Hark the Herald Angels Sing!* states this point:

> Veiled in flesh the Godhead see,
> Hail the incarnate Deity!
> Pleased as man with man to dwell,
> Jesus our Emmanuel!

The full force of this idea and its meaning for our understanding of God and ourselves, will become clear in the following chapter. In the present chapter, we are going to ask whether this idea is a reasonable summary of the New Testament evidence concerning Jesus, and look at the ways in which the Christian church has tried to express it.

Jesus as God

The resurrection had a decisive influence on Christian thinking about the identity and significance of Jesus. The theme of the risen life pervades the New Testament, and governs much of the early Christian proclamation. Thus Paul states that the resurrection established that Jesus was the Son of God (Romans 1:3–4). But did Jesus become the Son of God at his resurrection, or did the resurrection disclose something which had always been true? Did the resurrection change Jesus' status, or did it just make clear what that status had always been?

The New Testament regarded Jesus as having the status of the Son of God before his resurrection. Paul clearly regards Jesus as having this status at the time of his death, speaking of the 'Son of God, who loved me, and gave himself for me' (Galatians 2:20). The Synoptic Gospels indicate that Jesus enjoyed this status at least from the time of the beginning of his ministry (e.g. Mark 1:11). At some points, it even seems to be suggested that Jesus possessed this divine status from the beginning of time (John 1:1–14; Philippians 2:6–11; Colossians 1:15–20). At the very least, the New Testament indicates that there never was a time in his life that he was not already what the resurrection disclosed him to be – the Son of God. The resurrection demonstrated or proved Jesus' divine status in his lifetime. It was the clue to his identity and significance which clinched the case for his claim to a unique relationship to God. Let us look at some ways in which the New Testament expresses the divinity of Jesus.

We have noted two different ways of understanding Jesus, one based upon establishing what he achieved, and the other on who he was. The first of these two approaches is sometimes referred to as *functional*, and the second as an *ontological* Christology. A functional Christology is basically a way of thinking about Jesus which is primarily concerned with establishing what Jesus *did* – his 'function'. An ontological Christology is primarily concerned with establishing who Jesus *is* – in other words, his identity. These two ways of thinking about Jesus are virtually the same, in terms of their practical results. If Jesus is God, then he *acts as God and for* God. If Jesus *acts as God and for* God, then to all intents and purposes he *is* God. This is not a usurped authority, as if Jesus was claiming to act as and for God without due authorization. We are talking about Jesus being authorized to speak and act on behalf of God, something which is anticipated in his ministry and is finally confirmed by his being raised from the dead and being seated at the right hand of God.

An example of this is provided in Mark's account of how Jesus healed a paralytic (Mark 2:1–12). Jesus tells the paralytic that his sins are forgiven, to the outrage and astonishment of the Jewish teachers of the law watching him. 'He's blaspheming! Who can forgive sins but God alone!' (Mark 2:7). Those teachers were right. Only God can forgive sin. Unless Jesus was God, he had no authority whatsoever to speak those words. Yet Jesus declares that he does have such authority to forgive, and proceeds to heal the man (Mark 2:10–11). The resurrection of Jesus finally demonstrated conclusively that Jesus had the right to act in this way, retrospectively validating his claims to authority on earth.

The New Testament writers seem to have begun establishing the identity and significance of Jesus by reflecting on what he achieved, and then going on to ask who he must be if he is able to act in this way. This does not mean that the New Testament avoids direct statements about the identity of Jesus: we have already noted how it explicitly refers to Jesus as 'Messiah', 'Son of God' and 'God'. Rather, it is to note that the New Testament is especially interested in establishing what it was that Jesus did for us, and what this tells us about him. The good news of Jesus principally concerns what he has done for us. Having grasped this good news, we may then move on to reflect on the identity of the one who has made such great benefits available to us.

For this reason, it will be clear that there is no tension between 'functional' and 'ontological' under-standings of Jesus in the New Testament. There seems to have been a progression from statements concerning what Jesus achieved to statements about who he is. The first Christians found themselves obliged to speak of Jesus in divine terms, or at least terms which implied divinity, and thus to go on from there and think through the consequences of these ways of speaking about Jesus for their understanding of the relationship of Jesus to God. They had to answer this question: who must Jesus be if we are entitled to speak of him acting in this way? What must be true about Jesus if he truly reveals God? Who must he be if he is really able to redeem us? To make this point clearer, we shall explore some ways in which this interaction can be seen in the New Testament.

Jesus saves

The New Testament leaves us in no doubt that Jesus is our Saviour. Jesus is the 'Saviour, who is Christ the Lord' (Luke 2:11). In the third part of this book, we shall be exploring this theme in more detail, and look at some of the questions which it raises. For example, what does 'save' mean? And how is 'salvation' related to Jesus' life, death and resurrection? But we can already make a very important statement even at this stage. Only God can save! This theme is echoed throughout the Old Testament. Israel is regularly reminded that she cannot save herself, nor can she be saved by the idols of the nations round about her. It is the Lord, and the Lord alone, who will save. This point is made with special force in some of the prophetic writings, such as Isaiah 45:21–22:

Who foretold this long ago,
who declared it from the distant past?
Was it not I, the Lord?
And there is no God apart from me,
a righteous God and a Saviour;
there is none but me.
Turn to me and be saved, all you ends of the earth;
for I am God, and there is no other.

In the full knowledge that it was the Lord God alone who was Saviour, and that no other God could save, the first Christians had no hesitation in affirming that Jesus was Saviour – that Jesus could save. This was no misunderstanding on the part of people ignorant of the Old Testament tradition. It was a firm statement of who Jesus had to be, in the light of what he achieved through his saving death and resurrection.

One of the earliest symbols of faith used by Christians was a fish. The use of this symbol may partly reflect the fact that the first disciples were fishermen. But the real reason is that the five Greek letters spelling out 'fish' in Greek (I–CH–TH–U–S) are an acronym of the Christian slogan 'Jesus Christ, Son of God, Saviour'. In the New Testament, Jesus saves his people from their sins (Matthew 1:21); in his name alone is there salvation (Acts 4:12); he is the 'author of their salvation' (Hebrews 2:10). And in these affirmations, and countless others, Jesus is understood to function as God, doing something which, properly speaking, only God can do.

Jesus is worshipped
In the Jewish context within which the first Christians operated, it was God *and God alone* who is to be worshipped. The Second Commandment explicitly prohibited

135

the worship of anything and anyone other than the Lord God (Exodus 20:4–6). As Paul reminded the Christians at Rome, there was a constant danger that people would worship creatures, when they ought to be worshipping their Creator (Romans 1:23). We have already noted the early Christian church worshipped Christ as God – a practice which is clearly reflected in the New Testament. Thus 1 Corinthians 1:2 suggests that Christians are those who 'call upon the name of our Lord Jesus Christ', using language which reflects the Old Testament formulas for worshipping or adoring God (such as Genesis 4:26; 13:4; Psalm 105:1; Jeremiah 10:25 and Joel 2:32). Jesus is clearly understood to function as God, in that he is an object of worship.

Given the strict monotheism of the Jewish context within which this worship took place, it is clear that a crucial statement concerning Jesus' identity and significance is being made. The first Christians were well-informed Jews who were perfectly aware that there was only one God, and that it was utterly unacceptable to worship anyone other than God. These vitally important declarations were an integral part of their mental and spiritual world. Yet, in the full knowledge of all these things, they had no hesitation in speaking of Jesus Christ in terms which at least implied, and at times explicitly stated, he was God. This was no accident or misunderstanding. This was a deliberate and informed decision on the part of people who knew both their Jewish context and the astonishing history of Jesus Christ, culminating in his resurrection.

Jesus reveals God
'Anyone who has seen me has seen the Father' (John 14:9). These remarkable words, so characteristic of John's

gospel, emphasize that God the Father speaks and acts in the Son. God is revealed through, in and by Jesus. The Christian claim that God is most fully and authentically revealed in the face of Jesus Christ is simply a summary statement of the kaleidoscope of New Testament descriptions of the intimate relation between the Father and the Son, between God and Jesus. To have seen Jesus is to have seen the Father – in other words, Jesus is understood, once more, to function as God.

This point is stated clearly by the Swiss theologian Karl Barth (1886–1968), widely regarded as one of the greatest theological writers of the twentieth century. For Barth, Jesus is the key to an understanding of who God is and what he is like:

> When Holy Scripture speaks of God, it does not permit us to let our attention or thoughts wander at random . . . When Holy Scripture speaks of God, it concentrates our attention and thoughts upon one single point and what is to be known at that point . . . If we ask further concerning the one point upon which, according to Scripture, our attention and thoughts should and must be concentrated, then from first to last the Bible directs us to the name of Jesus Christ.

Jesus represents God

One of the great themes of the New Testament is that the promises of the Old Testament are fulfilled in the coming of Christ. The promises made by God to his people are seen to have been honoured. But the New Testament also contains promises, made by Jesus himself on behalf of God. For example, at the heart of the proclamation of the gospel as we find it in John's gospel lie the great prom ises of salvation: Anyone 'who believes has everlasting life' (John 6:47); 'Whoever eats my flesh and drinks my blood has eternal life, and I will raise him up at the last day' (John 6:54). According to John's gospel, Jesus makes promises on behalf of God. He is the plenipotentiary, the authorized representative, of God.

This idea is expressed particularly well by the Hebrew idea of the *shaliach* ('plenipotentiary'). The background to this idea lies in the concept of kingship found in the ancient world, particularly the ideas of delegation and representation on the part of the king in foreign regions. When a king sent his *shaliach* to negotiate with someone, that *shaliach* was empowered to act on his behalf – to enter into agreements, to make promises, and so on. Although the king was not himself physically present in these negotiations, to all intents and purposes he might just as well have been. The promises made are made on his behalf, and will be honoured by him. It is important to notice how often we find reference in John's gospel to the total unity of purpose of Father and Son (John 17:20–25): the Son is sent by the Father (John 6:57; 17:3), and acts on behalf of the Father (John 5:30). Jesus is clearly understood to make such promises on behalf of God, and at the desire of God, and is thus unquestionably understood as *functioning as God and for God* in this respect. Jesus functions as God's *shaliach*, his plenipotentiary representative, in whom and through whom God has pledged himself to act.

This does not mean that Jesus is merely a representative of God, or that God deals with us at second-hand, by sending someone to us on his behalf, and not coming to us himself. We are making a statement about the function of Jesus, which needs to be seen in the light of many other considerations about his function and identity.

Jesus functions as the authorized representative of God. But in the light of many other considerations, he is seen, not merely to *represent*, but to *be*, God. God deals with us at first-hand by coming among us in Christ.

It will be clear, on the basis of our discussion so far, that the New Testament at the very least understands Jesus to act as God and for God in every area of crucial relevance to Christianity. In short, we must learn to 'think about Jesus as we do about God' (to quote the second letter of Clement, a late first-century Christian writing which was greatly valued by the early church.) We are thus in a position to take the crucial step which underlies all Christian thinking on the incarnation – and that is to say that, as Jesus acts as God and for God in every context of importance, we should conclude that, for all intents and purposes, Jesus is God.

The implications of this will be clear. When we worship Jesus, we worship God; when we know Jesus, we know God; when we hear the promises of Jesus, we hear the promises of God; when we encounter Jesus, we encounter none other than the living God. The idea of the incarnation is the climax of Christian reflection upon the mystery of Christ – the recognition that Jesus revealed God; that Jesus represented God; that Jesus speaks as God and for God; that Jesus acted as God and for God; that Jesus *was* God. Yet the statement that Jesus is God adds nothing to the New Testament witness to Jesus. It merely brings together the totality of its testimony to the figure who stands at its centre.

Let us return once more to the resurrection. We have already seen that the New Testament recognizes that Jesus always was what the resurrection disclosed him to be. The resurrection established his divine status as Son of God. But where did this status come from? It is at this point that the close relationship between the resurrection and incarnation becomes clear. If Jesus Christ always possessed his unique status, that status must be traced back to his birth, and even further. The incarnation may thus be seen as the logical conclusion of Christian thinking concerning the significance of the resurrection.

Recently, there has been some discussion about the logical order of the incarnation and resurrection. One of the disadvantages of not being God is that we see things the wrong way round, looking at things from our standpoint, rather than God's. The order in which things actually exist (the 'order of being', as it is sometimes called) is usually exactly the opposite of the order in which we come to know about them (the 'order of knowing'). We come to know about Christ's divinity through the resurrection, and as a result, we arrive at the idea of the incarnation. So we could say that the resurrection comes before the incarnation in the 'order of knowing'. But it will be obvious that, once we know about the incarnation, we realize that it must take precedence over the resurrection in the 'order of being'. We could summarize this by saying that Christ was divine before the resurrection discloses that he is divine. But this argument is not particularly important: all that we need to note here is that there is a very close relationship between the incarnation and resurrection.

Making sense of Jesus as God

The problem that the Christian church now had to deal with was simply this: how could Jesus be both divine and human, God and man? We have already explored the evidence and thinking which lay behind this conclusion; the problem which now emerged was to make sense of it! How could it be conceptualized? The first four or five centuries saw this question being debated at great length throughout the Christian world.

In many respects, the debates are of little interest for our purposes, concerning technical matters of Greek philosophy of little relevance for today. But they are important in one respect – they show how well aware the church was that the gospel itself was at stake in these debates. For the early Christian writers, Jesus had to be both God and a human being if salvation was to be a possibility. If Jesus was not God, he could not save; if Jesus was not human, he could not save us. The affirmation that Jesus Christ was both God and a human being came to be seen as a means of safeguarding the gospel proclamation of the redemption of humanity in Christ. Jesus saves us. As only God can save, Jesus must be God. And as Jesus is a human being, he is able to make salvation available to us. Jesus thus mediates salvation from God to us on account of being both God and human. Only God incarnate could act in this way.

The early Christians were actually far more interested in defending this insight, than trying to explain it! We must never fall into the trap of suspecting that the early Christian writers thought that they were explaining how Jesus could be both God and a human being. It is clear that they were simply trying to find ways of making sense of a mystery, something which in the end defied explanation. But it was no mystery invented just to give bishops or theologians something to do with their spare time. It was the central mystery of the Christian faith, upon which Christianity would stand or fall.

To illustrate this point, let us leave the first five centuries of the Christian era behind for a moment, and move to a very different situation – Berlin in the early nineteenth century. At this point, Berlin was the capital city of Prussia, one of the most important German states. A university had been established in the city, and had rapidly achieved pre-eminence, attracting brilliant philosophers such as Hegel to its faculties. One of its most distinguished theologians was Friedrich D. E. Schleiermacher, one of the more important Christian thinkers of the last two centuries. Like many people at the time, Schleiermacher found the 'doctrine of the two natures' rather heavy going. On the one hand, it seemed difficult to understand; on the other hand, it seemed to him that it was absolutely necessary. Why? Let us follow his reasoning through.

Christians believe that we are saved only through Jesus Christ. (That is a rather bald summary of the many statements of the New Testament on the matter, but it is good enough for our purposes). What does this actually imply? The first point that Schleiermacher makes is this. It is obvious that Jesus is a man, a human being in some ways like the rest of us. That point does not really need to be emphasized, but it is a good point from which to start our thinking. But if he is *just* a human being, like all the rest of us, we find ourselves faced with a problem. For this would mean that he would share our need for redemption. As he would not be able to redeem us, he would turn out to be part of the problem, instead of a potential solution to it. So there must be some essential difference between Jesus and the rest of us, if Jesus is indeed to be our redeemer.

At first sight, it might seem that we could avoid this problem by getting rid of the idea that Jesus is a human being altogether, and simply state that he is God. But then he would have no point of contact with those who need redemption. How can he relate to us? There must be some point of difference between Christ and God which allows Christ to make contact with those whom he is meant to redeem. So Jesus must be both God and human if he is able to redeem us. This simply states the basic principle which lies behind the idea of the incarnation. Dorothy L. Sayers stated this point memorably, in a lecture entitled 'Creed or Chaos?'. 'If Christ was only man, then he is entirely irrelevant to any thought about God; if he is only God, then he is entirely irrelevant to any experience of human life.'

Jesus as mediator
We could develop the same idea along different lines. Let us suppose that we are dealing with two individuals, who we shall call 'A' and 'B'. They enjoy a close relationship, which unfortunately breaks down completely over some misunderstanding. A is convinced that it is the fault of B, and B is sure that A is in the wrong. So strongly do they hold their views that they refuse to speak to each other. The situation is, unfortunately, all too familiar from everyday experience, whether it is a matter of personal relationships, industrial relations, or international diplomacy. We all know situations where this has happened, and may have been involved with them ourselves. But how can the situation be resolved? How can A and B become reconciled? The situation demands a mediator, a go-between.

The best mediator or go-between is someone who both A and B know and respect, but who will be impartial. Let us call this mediator 'C'. C must represent A to B, and B to A. He or she must not be identified with either A or B, yet must have points of contact with both in order to be accepted by both sides. This situation is familiar to us all. It's just a question of working out who C must be.

Late Victorian novels often portray a crisis arising between a father and his son, with the mother acting as the mediator between them. Although she is not identical with either father or son, she has relationships with both of them which establish her credentials as a go-between. She is close enough to each of them to represent them both, and yet sufficiently different from them both to prevent her being identified with either. The relevance of this little digression for our understanding of the identity of Jesus Christ will be obvious.

The idea of Jesus being the one and only go-between or mediator between God and us is deeply embedded in the New Testament. 'For there is one God, and there is one mediator between God and humanity, Jesus Christ' (1 Timothy 2:5). Paul talks about God 'reconciling' us to himself through Jesus Christ (2 Corinthians 5:18–19). What is particularly interesting is that in this passage Paul uses exactly the same Greek word to refer to the restoration of the relationship between God and humanity which he had used earlier to refer to the restoration of the relationship between a man and his wife who had become alienated in some manner (1 Corinthians 7:10–11). Christ is clearly understood to act as the mediator or go-between, restoring the relation between God and humanity to what it once was.

A mediator must represent God to us, and us to God. The mediator must have points of contact with both God and us, and yet be distinguishable from both. In short, the traditional idea of the incarnation, which expresses the belief that Jesus is both divine and human, portrays Jesus as the perfect mediator between God and ourselves. Christ is like us in every way, except that he does not share our need to be redeemed. He possesses a unique ability to redeem us, on account of his identity as the Son of God. He is thus able to relate to us on the one hand, and redeem us on the other.

The Council of Chalcedon

How, then, may the idea that Jesus is God be understood? The exhaustive discussion in the first five centuries of the precise relationship between Christ, God and humanity was brought to an end by the Council of Chalcedon (AD 451). Just as a person chairing a committee finally feels obliged to bring a seemingly endless debate to a conclusion when all the issues appear to have been raised and exhaustively discussed (only to be raised again!), so the Council of Chalcedon was convened to bring the debate within the early church on the identity of Jesus Christ to an end. (In fact, debate would continue for centuries to come; however, Chalcedon remained a definitive reference point and milestone in those later debates.)

Over five hundred bishops met to hammer out an agreement which would do justice to the various points which had been established during the course of the debate. The Christian church in Alexandria (a city in modern-day Egypt) had laid stress upon the importance of the divinity of Christ, whereas the church in Antioch (a city in modern-day Turkey) had laid much greater emphasis upon the humanity of Christ. All sorts of theories had been put forward to explain the way in which God and humanity were united in Christ. Which would the Council adopt?

What the Council actually said is very significant. It did not lay down one specific way of thinking about the relationship between Jesus, God and humanity. Instead, it stated that it was necessary to regard Jesus Christ as fully divine and fully human. Christ is *vere Deus et vere homo*, 'true God and true man', a statement which is often referred to as the 'Chalcedonian Definition'. In doing this, the Council was simply restating what was widely agreed within the church: that if Jesus was not God, he had no bearing upon any thought about God; and if he was not human, he had no bearing upon human life. It merely restated a crucially important insight; it did not explain it, or lay down some specific way of making sense of it. But this was all that the Council wanted to do: identify the essential point at issue.

The Council may be regarded as laying down a controlling principle for classical Christology, which has been accepted ever since as definitive within Christian thinking concerning the identity and significance of Jesus Christ. The principle in question could be summarized like this: provided that it is recognized that Jesus Christ is both truly divine and truly human, the exact way in which this is articulated or explored is not of fundamental importance. Oxford patristic scholar Maurice Wiles summarized Chalcedon's aims as follows:

> On the one hand was the conviction that a saviour must be fully divine; on the other was the conviction that what is not assumed is not healed. Or, to put the matter in other words, the source of salvation must be God; the locus of salvation must be humanity. It is quite clear that these two principles often pulled in opposite directions. The Council of Chalcedon was the church's attempt to resolve, or perhaps rather to agree to live with, that tension. Indeed, to accept both principles as strongly as did the early church is already to accept the Chalcedonian faith.

146

Chalcedon was content to reaffirm a fact, without attempting to offer a binding interpretation of it – and it was wise to do so. Interpretations vary from one age to another, depending upon the time and place. Thus Platonism might be used to interpret the doctrine of the incarnation in third-century Alexandria, Aristotelianism in thirteenth-century Paris, and Hegelianism in nineteenth-century Berlin. In every case, a prevailing philosophical system is drawn upon to illuminate aspects of the doctrine. But philosophies go out of date, whereas the doctrine of the incarnation does not. The truth expressed by the doctrine – that God has entered into and made possible a transformation of our human existence – remains constant, whatever additional ideas or concepts we may make use of in explaining it to our intellectually sophisticated contemporaries. Christianity has never become enslaved to any one philosophy. To give an example: you can be a Christian and a Hegelian, yet do not have to be a Hegelian to become a Christian.

Chalcedon did not commit itself to any one philosophical system or outlook which would probably have been abandoned as outdated within centuries, and been an embarrassment to the church ever afterwards. Rather, it attempted to safeguard an essential fact, which could be interpreted in terms of philosophical ideas or concepts which might make sense at any particular point in history, provided these explanations do not deny or explain away any part of the fact. As a result, Christian theologians and apologists have enjoyed a considerable degree of liberty in defending and explaining this central Christian doctrine to different audiences throughout Christian history.

Every explanation of the person and work of Jesus Christ must, in the final analysis, be recognized to be inadequate, and Chalcedon merely stated with great clarity what the essential fact was which required explanation and interpretation: Jesus really is both God and a human being. So long as Jesus was recognized as being both God and a human being, all was well. So long as we know that we really do encounter God in Jesus, and not some demi-god or deluded egomaniac, we know that he has a unique position in relation to both God and ourselves, and may base our faith upon it. So long as we know that in Jesus we really do encounter a human being, we may rest assured that God is involved in human history and experience – and, specifically, in our own history and experience.

To make this point absolutely clear, the Council used a technical term, already well-established by this time. This is the Greek term *homoousios*, which is usually translated into English as 'of one substance', or 'of one being'. Jesus is 'of one substance' with God, just as he is 'of one substance' with us. In other words, Jesus is the *same* as God; it really is God himself who we encounter in Jesus, and not some messenger sent from God. Although this term was not itself biblical, it was widely regarded as expressing a thoroughly biblical insight.

In the early church, a remarkably heated debate had developed over this term, and especially its advantages over a related term, which differed from it by only one letter. While *homoousios*, 'of the same substance', was widely accepted as being the orthodox position, some felt that the similar term *homoiousios*, 'of a similar substance', was more appropriate. In his famous book, *The Decline and Fall of the Roman Empire*, Edmund Gibbon pointed out that never before had so much fuss been made over a single letter of the alphabet. The Council unequivocally endorsed the view that Jesus was 'of the

148

same substance' as God. Jesus was not just like God; he was God.

It might seem that this debate was somewhat pointless. But there is all the difference in the world between the two ideas. If Jesus is only 'similar to' God, we encounter someone who is like God, at least in some way. It is not God himself who we encounter, but someone who is like him. God sends his troubleshooter, and keeps out of things himself. God remains aloof from human history and human experience, he experiences us at second hand, and vice versa. The vital direct link between God and Jesus is broken. God does not speak to us directly; he simply sends his representative. God would not know what it is like to be frail, weak, and mortal. He would not know what it is like to be human, like ourselves. If Jesus is only like God, we can approach God as someone whom we know only indirectly, and, to make matters even worse, who knows us only indirectly.

At Chalcedon, the church opted conclusively for a different understanding of the relation of Jesus and God. Jesus is God. In Jesus, we encounter God at first hand, directly. To encounter the risen Christ is to encounter none other than the living and loving God. To put this in a dangerously crude way: God knows what it is like to be human. Although only a single letter separates *homoiousios* ('being like God') from *homoousios* ('being the same as God'), a world separates the views of Jesus which they represent. In English, the difference might be brought out by saying that the former corresponds to JESUS IS GOOD and the latter to JESUS IS GOD. They differ only by a letter, and yet by everything, as will become clear in the following chapters. Chalcedon made no attempt to explain the mystery with which we are confronted as Christians, and we totally misrepresent

149

and misunderstand them if we think they did. They just identified the central point at stake, and made crystal clear the Christian point of view.

Chalcedon simply states definitively what the first five centuries of Christian reflection on the New Testament had already established. It defines the point from which we start – the recognition that, in the face of Christ, we see none other than God himself. That is a starting point, not an end. But we must be sure of our starting point, the place at which we begin, if the result is to be reliable. Chalcedon claims to have established that starting point, and whatever difficulties we may find with its turgid language and outdated expressions, the basic ideas which it lays down are clear and crucial, and are obviously a legitimate interpretation of the New Testament witness to Jesus Christ.

What happens when we move on from this starting point? What are the results of believing that Jesus is both God and a human being? What does the doctrine of the incarnation tell us about God and about ourselves? What does it tell us about the nature of God, and our own destiny? In short: what is the cash value of the incarnation? Let us move on and see.

8

Jesus as God: its significance

Jesus is God – that is the basic meaning of the doctrine of the incarnation. It is a remarkably profound and exciting idea, which has enormous consequences for the way in which we think about ourselves and about God. In this chapter, we are going to 'unpack' the meaning of the belief that Jesus is both God and and human. Some of the ideas it involves are simple, others are more complex.

The maleness of Jesus

How important is it that Jesus was a man? As we have already seen, this is of vital importance. If Jesus was not truly human, he would have no point of contact with us. He would be a stranger to the human situation. We would not be able to relate to him. Those points were explored in the previous chapter. But there is a deeper issue here. How important is it that Jesus was *male*? Many women wonder if they are somehow disadvantaged by the fact that God chose to become incarnate as a male, rather than a female. In view of the importance of this issue, we will explore it a little, before moving on to other issues.

The gospel centres on a series of central affirmations. Anyone who believes in Jesus Christ will have eternal life. Whoever calls upon the name of the Lord will be saved. Anyone who repents of their sins will be forgiven. These promises are made to all, irrespective of gender or nationality. They are grounded in what God achieved in and through Jesus Christ. The doctrine of the incarnation declares that God enters into our human situation, sharing its sorrows and griefs, in order to transform that situation. God chose to become human, in order that we might be reconciled to him. To put it crudely, this entailed either becoming a male or a female. But the *particularity* of the gender of the redeemer does not in any way imply a corresponding limitation on the scope of redemption. Christ was a Jew; he died to redeem both Jews and Gentiles. Christ was a male; he died to redeem both males and females. Jesus was an Aramaic-speaker who brings salvation to those who spoke or speak Aramaic, Latin, English or Cantonese. His nationality, gender, blood group and hair colour have no bearing upon the scope of redemption. Equally, chronology has no bearing upon the scope of redemption. It is not simply those who were alive at the same time as Jesus who can be redeemed by him; the saving power of the risen Christ is both prospective and retrospective.

By choosing to enter into history as one of us, it was inevitable that God would commit himself to a set of specific historical circumstances in the incarnation. The incarnate God would possess a specific nationality, culture, gender, language, blood group, and hair colour. But the *particularities* of the incarnation must be set against the *universality* of the redemption which is thereby made possible. The central affirmation of the incarnation is that God became one of us in order to redeem us, not that he became a first-century male Palestinian Jew. No culture, gender, or language is given enhanced priority on account of the incarnation, nor can people of any culture, gender or language be regarded as 'second-class' Christians. With that point in mind, we may return to deal with the importance of the incarnation in relation to our knowledge of God.

The incarnation and knowing God

How do we discover what God is like in the first place? When Christians speak about God, they mean God as he has been revealed in Jesus Christ, the God who became incarnate. Jesus is like an authorized visual aid to understanding God. He is someone who is able and authorized to allow us to know what God is like. 'Anyone who has seen me has seen the Father' (John 14:9).

Realizing that Jesus Christ is God incarnate allows us to speak about God in positive, vivid and dynamic ways. Without Jesus, we could still say that God is immortal, invisible, infinite, and so on. But that is actually saying what God is *not* rather than what God *is*. It is to declare that God is *not* mortal, *not* visible and *not* finite. While all this may well be true, it is hardly very exciting or interesting. What can we say positively about God? It is here that the divinity of Christ establishes a crucial principle: *God is Christlike*. These three simple words can totally alter our way of thinking about God.

An example will make this clear. What can we say about the love of God for us? We could say that it is infinite, boundless, beyond human telling, and so on. Once more, however, all that we have done is to speak of it in purely negative terms. We would have explained what it is not, but failed to set out what it is. In fact, we would virtually be saying that, whatever the love of God

153

may be like, we can't say anything about it. But the love of God is a rather important and exciting aspect of Christianity, something which we would very much like to be able to talk about! Surely we can say something clear, intelligible, positive and exciting about it, unless we are doomed to have to keep quiet about it forever! On the basis of the divinity of Jesus, we may make a very positive and simple statement about the love of God for humanity. The love of God is like the love of a man who lays down his life for his friends (John 15:13). Immediately, we are given a picture, an image, drawn from human experience – something concrete and tangible, something we can visualize and relate to.

A picture is worth a thousand words. In the picture of someone laying down his life, giving his very being, for someone he loves, we have a most powerful, striking and moving statement of the full extent of the love of God for sinners. We can talk about the love of God in terms of our own experience, and supremely in terms of the tender image of Jesus Christ trudging to Calvary, there to die for those he loved. Jesus did not need to do this; he chose to do it. It is a moving, poignant and deeply evocative image, which we can easily imagine and identify with; in short, it is a statement about the love of God which speaks to us, which appeals to us, and which brings home exactly what the love of God is like. No longer need we be at a loss for words to speak about God. We are given a handle to attach to God, in order that we may get hold of him. One of the early Christian writers, Origen, compared the incarnation to a small statue – a scaled-down model of the real thing, which allows us to discern its features more clearly.

We could even say that until the coming of Christ, every image of God was ultimately an idol, in that it is something which we ourselves constructed and worshipped. In Christ, we are given an image of God – something we can visualize, imagine in our minds, and relate to. Yet this is an authorized picture of God. It is not one which we have invented or imagined; it is one which we have been given, and which we are expected to use. No longer need we be at a loss for words! We can speak of the love of God for all its worth as we focus on the death of Jesus on the cross.

This approach also allows us to avoid the unthinking sentimentality that sometimes finds its way into discussions of the love of God. Without the death of Christ, there is every danger that our conception of the love of God will be soft and mushy. The cross brings home the deep relationship of severity and kindness, already known to every parent, which is so characteristic of God's dealings with us. The appalling cost of forgiveness to God is shown in the cross. God does not simply say 'Never mind!' to the sinner, pretending that sin never happened or that it is of no significance. It is too easy for us to overlook the anger of God against human sin, and the great offence which it causes him. Nor can its horrific consequences for human existence be overlooked. The death of Christ tears away the mask from sin, and allows it to be seen for what it really is.

True forgiveness involves facing and recognizing the great pain and distress caused by the offence, a process for which the cross is perhaps the most powerful illustration known. The love of God for his people is expressed, not in a soft and sentimental way, but in the context of the seriousness and totality of God's hatred for sin. The cross sets forward the full and tremendous cost of real forgiveness in which the full seriousness of sin is met and dealt with, and its guilt purged through the death of the Son of God. The cross confronts us with the knowledge that our sin wounds God to the heart, causing more hurt than we can ever imagine. Yet God offers us forgiveness – a real, if painful, forgiveness, in which all is faced and all is forgiven, in order that we may go forth into eternal life with God. Recognition of sin is a humiliating, painful yet ultimately healing process. God humbled himself to meet us, and we must also humble ourselves if we are to meet him.

The incarnation makes God tangible. It helps us think about God in powerful and vivid ways. We could further unpack the meaning of the incarnation by thinking about two pieces of glass. The first is a window. Suppose you are in a room which is completely dark, without any means of letting light in. Then someone knocks a hole in the wall and makes a window. The light is let in and the room is illuminated. But we can also see the outside world through the window – a world which has always been there, but which we couldn't see properly before. Jesus is a window into God; he is the light of God who has come into the world to illuminate it, and who lets us see God. Perhaps the window is not as large and the glass less clear than we would like (1 Corinthians 13:12 is worth noting here), but God is suddenly made available for us in a new way. Many of us know what it is like to get up early in the morning, stepping out of bed into a dark room. When we open the curtains, the room is suddenly flooded with light and the outside world beckons to us. The same sense of excitement, like a dark room being flooded with light, or a beautiful landscape opening up before our eyes, can perhaps be felt when reading the opening sections of John's gospel (John 1:1–18), and other biblical passages dealing with the divinity of Jesus.

The second piece of glass is a mirror. As we look in a mirror, we see ourselves reflected. As we look at Christ, we see ourselves as we shall finally be – people in a perfect relationship with God. Jesus discloses to us what it is like to be truly human, to live with God and for God. As we look at him, we are made painfully aware of just how far we have to go before we are anything like him! But the vision of restored and redeemed humanity presented in Jesus Christ gives us a foretaste of the New Jerusalem, an encouragement as we try to grow more like him and a challenge to our commitment to the gospel which alone can transform us in this way. Two pieces of glass; two aspects of Jesus Christ.

It is quite astonishing how some people discuss the question 'Is Christ divine?' as if they already had an excellent idea about what God is like, while Christ himself remains something of an enigma. But exactly the opposite is so obviously the case! Christ confronts us through the gospel narratives and through experience, whereas we have no clear vision of God. As John's gospel reminds us: 'No-one has ever seen God, but God the One and Only, who is at the Father's side, has made him known' (John 1:18). God is Christlike. We learn to think of God as we see him in Christ. For the Christian, it is Christ who provides us with the basis of the most reliable knowledge of God available.

All too often, critics of the incarnation dismiss the idea because it seems inconsistent with their understanding of God. It is quite astonishing, however, how these critics seem to know exactly what God is like, and on the basis of this idea of God, reject the incarnation. But on what basis do they establish this idea of God? What source of knowledge do they possess which is denied to everyone else, and which is more reliable than the knowledge of God to be had in Jesus Christ? Criticisms of the incarnation often seem to boil down to the simple, and not very significant, statement that someone somewhere has a preconceived idea of God which is inconsistent with the idea of the incarnation. So what? Where does that preconceived idea come from? Unless that person can prove, beyond all reasonable doubt, that God is really like that, the criticism is not important. And on what basis would such a person be able to make such a statement? He or she must have some kind of special revelation from God, a kind of personal hot line to heaven denied to everyone else, to be able to make such an arrogant and presumptuous statement! Yet this criticism, flawed though it is, does allow us to appreciate a vital point: we need to be told what God is like.

The simple fact is that humanity has been unable to reach much agreement on what God is like, or how many gods there are anyway, even after a couple of thousand years of argument. For the Christian, God is to be known and seen most reliably as we encounter him in Jesus Christ. That may be inconsistent with somebody else's view of God – but that doesn't entitle them to say that the Christian view of God, expressed in the incarnation, is wrong. All statements about God are ultimately a matter of faith (even those of the atheist!), and the most that such critics can do is register their disagreement with the Christian viewpoint. To do more is to go far beyond the limited evidence available at their disposal.

People have tried to think about the nature of God for some considerable time, without reaching much agreement. A philosopher in the classical theist tradition would regard the word 'God' as referring to some supreme absolute, about which we can say rather little.

It was against this idea of God that the French philosopher Blaise Pascal protested when he wrote his famous words: 'the God of Abraham, Isaac and Jacob, not of the philosophers'. The deist would regard God as a heavenly watchmaker who, having wound up the universe and set it going, left it to its own devices. Many Hindus would feel able to say, without the slightest sense of impropriety, '*I* am God' – meaning that the one unchanging reality is spread among all existing things to such an extent that it can't be separated from any of them. Other Hindus would want to talk about a variety of gods, each occupying a different place in their pantheon. Some of them are quite happy to add Jesus Christ to this collection of deities, providing he doesn't displace anyone important. The atheist would treat the word 'God' as referring to a remote supernatural ruler (who doesn't exist anyway) who hurls down arbitrary dictates to humanity from a distant Olympus, and imprisons the human spirit in time and space. And so on. We could give an exhaustive list of the various ideas about God which humanity has toyed around with since we began to think, but there would be little point in doing so. All that we want to make clear is that the word 'God' can mean any number of things. In countries where Christianity has been dominant, of course, this difficulty may be less important than we have suggested. But it obviously raises the question: What God are we actually talking about? How do we know what 'God' is like? Where can we find out?

All sorts of answers have been given to questions like these. God may be seen in a glorious sunset, in the night sky, in the ordering of the universe, to name but three answers to one of them ('Where can we see God?'). The Christian insists that God is to be most reliably and completely known as he is revealed in the person of Jesus Christ. This is not to say that God may not be known, in various ways and to various degrees, by other means. Christians believe that Jesus Christ is the closest encounter with God to be had in this life. God makes himself available for our acceptance or rejection in the figure of Jesus Christ. To have encountered Jesus is to have encountered God. Paul refers to Jesus as the 'image of the invisible God' (Colossians 1:15). In the letter to the Hebrews, we find Jesus Christ described as the 'exact representation' of God's nature (Hebrews 1:3). The Greek word used here could refer to an image stamped upon a coin, conveying the idea of an exact representation of a ruler or monarch. The God with whom we are dealing is the 'God and Father of our Lord Jesus Christ' (1 Peter 1:3), the God who seeks us, finds us and meets us in Jesus Christ.

On 'knowing God' and 'knowing about God'
What sorts of things does the incarnation tell us about the 'God and Father of our Lord Jesus Christ'? Perhaps most obviously, it tells us that God is no distant ruler who remains aloof from the affairs of his creatures, but is passionately concerned with them to the extent that he takes the initiative in coming to them. God doesn't just reveal things *about* himself – he reveals *himself* in Jesus Christ. Revelation is personal. It is not simply given in a set of propositions, a list of statements which we are meant to accept, but in a person. It is to Christ, and not to the creed, that the world must look for redemption. Like a signpost, the creed points away from itself to the one hope of redemption, Jesus Christ. It is not the creed, but the astonishing act of God in history to which it bears witness, which is the source of the saving power

underlying the Christian proclamation. Christianity has always insisted that we can *know* – not just *know about* – God. God does not encounter us as an abstract lifeless idea, but as a living person.

We may know a lot about the President of the United States, or the British Royal Family – but that does not mean that we actually know them. The fact that I have read one of the countless books about a famous member of the royal family may mean that I know a lot about them; but it does not mean that I know them. For someone to be known means that they want to be known – there must be a willingness on their part to let us know them. There is a sense in which every personal relationship is based upon *grace* – that is, a free decision on the part of one person that they wish to be known by another. As every college student who has ever fallen in love knows only too well, wanting to get to know someone does not necessarily mean that this feeling is reciprocated!

There is, however, more to the gospel than God being prepared to be known by us. That could be taken to imply that we take the initiative, seeking him out, and knocking on his door. Yet the gospel declares that it is God who takes the initiative in approaching us, in disclosing to us that he wants us to know him. God reveals himself to us, and by revealing himself, discloses his love for us and his desire to enter into a relationship with us. Christianity is not about our search for God; it is about God's search for us.

The doctrine of the incarnation speaks to us of a God who acts to demonstrate his love for us. That 'God is love' (1 John 4:8) is a deep and important truth – but far more important is the truth that God acted to demonstrate this love. 'This is how God showed his love among us: He sent his one and only Son into the world that we might live through him' (1 John 4:9).

Actions, as we are continually reminded, speak louder than words. The statement that 'God is love' could easily be misunderstood as a static, timeless universal truth; that 'God so loved the world that he gave his one and only Son, that whoever believes in him shall not perish but have eternal life' (John 3:16), makes it clear that God is dynamic, a living God, who does things in order to reveal the full extent of his love for us.

God humbles himself in order to make himself known to us, to call us back to him, to reveal the full extent of his love towards us. That is one of the most wonderful insights the doctrine of the incarnation has to offer us. So much does God love us, that he humbles himself, in order to bring us back to him. This great theme of the humility of God is central to many Christmas carols. Perhaps one of the finest and best-known statements of this theme of the self-humiliation of the redeemer is due to Mrs Cecil F. Alexander, in her carol *Once in Royal David's City*:

> He came down to earth from heaven
> Who is God and Lord of all
> And his shelter was a stable
> And his cradle was a stall.
> With the poor and mean and lowly
> Lived on earth our Saviour holy.

The theme of the humility of God is expounded with great feeling in a famous passage, usually thought to be a Christian hymn going back even before the writings of Paul, which Paul quotes (in much the same way as I have been quoting from hymns in this chapter):

> [Jesus Christ], being in very nature God, did not consider equality with God something to be grasped, but made himself nothing, taking the very nature of a servant, being made in human likeness. And being found in appearance as a man, he humbled himself and became obedient to death – even death on a cross! (Philippians 2:6–8).

This passage brings to mind many accounts of great men and women who humbled themselves to bring about something worthwhile. Many will know the story of the ancient king, who chose to leave a life of luxury in his palace, and live as a peasant among his people, in order to understand them and thus rule them better on his return. So God stoops down in order to meet us where we are.

Christianity does not teach that we have to climb a ladder into heaven in order to find God and be with him; rather, it declares that God has come down that ladder, in order to meet us where we are, and take us back with him. We don't have to become like God before we can encounter him, because God became like us first. God meets us right where we are, without preconditions. This point is brought out clearly in a famous saying of Athanasius: 'God became human so that we might become God'. By this, Athanasius meant that God became a human being in order that we might enter into a relationship and fellowship with him. The personal relationship which Christians presently enjoy with God through Christ is a foretaste of the fuller and deeper fellowship we will one day enjoy.

God is with us

One of the greatest insights of the doctrine of the incarnation is that God himself enters into the world, the vale of soul-making, full of darkness and tragedy. It is this 'far country' into which the Father enters, to call his lost children home. Let us remind ourselves of one of the great opening statements of John's gospel: 'The Word became flesh, and made his dwelling among us' (John 1:14). The Greek word translated 'made his dwelling' could be translated more accurately as 'pitched his tent'. This translation presents us with a powerful image, undiminished by the passage of time. The image is that of a wandering people, who dwell in tents (as Israel once did, in the period looked back to by the prophets as a time when she was close to God). One day they awake to find a new tent pitched in their midst. God himself has come to dwell among them, as they wander. God is with them.

'God is with us'. This great theme of the incarnation is summed up in the name Immanuel (Matthew 1:20–23). We must appreciate the importance of names for the biblical writers. Being allowed to give someone a name established your authority over them. In the creation accounts, it is Adam who is allowed to name the animals (Genesis 2:19–20) and thus to establish authority over them. But no human being is allowed to name God. It is God himself who reveals his name to us (Exodus 3:13–15). We are not allowed to establish authority over God. To name someone is to claim authority over them, just as the Babylonians gave new names to Daniel and his companions to indicate they were servants of the state (Daniel 1:7). To name someone or something is to assert ownership or stewardship over them.

The name chosen was believed to indicate the nature

of the person being named. So it was with Jesus. Mary and Joseph are told what the name of their child shall be. They were not permitted to choose it themselves: 'you shall call his name Jesus, for he will save his people from their sins' (Matthew 1:21). Mary and Joseph did not choose this name, as if the idea of Jesus as a potential Saviour was their idea; the name was chosen for them, indicating that they were authorized to give the child this name, with all that this implied. The name 'Jesus' literally means 'God saves', just as 'Immanuel' means 'God with us' (Matthew 1:23).

What, then, does 'God being with us' mean? Two main meanings may be identified. First, God is on our side; secondly, God is present with us. 'If God is for us, who can be against us?' (Romans 8:31–32). 'God is with us' means 'God is on our side'. The birth of the Son of God demonstrates and proclaims that God is on our side, that he has committed himself to the cause of the salvation of sinful humanity. In the birth of the long-promised Saviour, in his death on the cross of Calvary, and in his resurrection from the dead we have a demonstration, a proof, a guarantee, that God stands by us. Christmas tells us that the God we are dealing with, the God and Father of our Lord Jesus Christ, is not a God who is indifferent to our fate, but one who is passionately committed to our salvation, to redeeming us from sin, and to raising us to eternal life on the last day.

Secondly, 'God is with us' means that God is present among us. We are not talking of a God who stands far off from his world, aloof and distant from its problems. We are dealing with a God who has entered into our human situation, who became man and dwelt among us as one of us, someone who knows at first hand what it is like to be frail, mortal and human, to suffer and to die.

We cannot explain suffering, but we can say that God chose to suffer alongside us. At the scene of the crucifixion, the crowds standing around Jesus made fun of him. Even the soldiers sneered at him. 'If you are the king of the Jews,' they said, 'save yourself' (Luke 23:37). But he stayed there and died, and saved us instead. One of the greatest wonders of the gospel is that God chose to save us by suffering himself.

Christ the wounded physician

God suffered in Christ. He knows what it is like to be human – an astonishing, and comforting, thought. We are not talking about God becoming like us, just as if he was putting on some sort of disguise so that he could be passed off as one of us. We are talking about the God who created the world entering into that same world as one of us and on our behalf, in order to redeem us. God has not sent a messenger or a representative to help the poor creatures that we are; he has involved himself directly, redeeming his own creation, instead of getting someone else to do it for him. God is not like a general who issues orders to his troops from the safety of a bomb-proof shelter, miles away from the front line, but one who leads his troops from the front, having previously done all that he asks them to do in turn.

Suffering is a real problem for many people. Time and time again, we have been promised solutions which will eliminate pain and suffering from the world. All will be well – that is, once we have adopted some new social policy, or improved our economic throughput, or made further advances in drug research. Somehow, the promises keep on coming, and there is no sign of the sorrow of the world being alleviated. It seems to be here to stay. So what can be said to a suffering world?

In the history of the world, four main answers have been given to this question. First, suffering is real, and is not going to go away. However, we can take comfort from the fact that life does not go on for ever. In the end, we will die, and once we are dead, suffering ends and we have eventual peace. Secondly, suffering is an illusion. It simply is not there, but is imagined. If we concentrate hard enough, the illusion will vanish. Thirdly, suffering is real. However, it is something that intelligent peope ought to be able to rise above, and recognize that it is of little importance. Each of these seems to have little to offer the world, often requiring a suspension of disbelief rather than leading to a cessation of suffering.

The Christian has the fourth answer: God suffered in Christ. God knows what it is like to suffer. The letter to the Hebrews talks about Jesus being our 'sympathetic High Priest' (Hebrews 4:15) – someone who suffers along with us (which is the literal meaning of both the Greek word *sympathetic* and the Latin word *compassionate*). This does not explain suffering, although it may make it more tolerable to bear. It expresses the deep insight that God himself suffered at first hand as we suffer. We are given a new perspective on life. Christianity has always held that it is the suffering of Christ upon the cross which is the culmination, the climax, of his ministry. God the creator enters into his creation – not as a curious tourist, but as a committed Saviour. He did not need to suffer to know what it was like. He chose to suffer as a public demonstration that he knows suffering at first hand. God knows how weak our faith is, and does all he can to sustain and support it from his side. The suffering of Jesus Christ is meant to reassure us that we have the privilege of relating to a God who knows the pain and

167

sorrow of living in a fallen world. The passion stories of the gospels tell of a Saviour who really understands suffering, and who has been through it himself.

There is a famous saying about the medical profession: 'Only the wounded physician can heal'. Whether this is true or not is a matter for debate. But it does highlight the fact that we are able to relate better to someone who has shared our problem, who has been through what we are going through now – and triumphed over it. As many already know from experience, it is often difficult to relate to someone who hasn't shared our problem. One way of getting round this is the idea of 'empathy'. You empathize with the other person's problems and fears. Even though you haven't shared them – and may not even be able to understand them! – you try to think yourself into their situation, so that you can tell them that you understand exactly how they must be feeling. It works splendidly, provided the person you're trying to help doesn't start asking awkward questions, which expose your lack of first-hand experience of their situation! The incarnation speaks of God sympathizing with our sufferings – not empathizing, as if he himself hadn't experienced them at first hand. God sympathizes, in the strict sense of 'suffers alongside', with us. In turning to God, we turn to one who knows and understands.

There is a splendid story told about medieval shepherds in East Anglia, which was then the centre of England's wool trade. During the later Middle Ages, a dead shepherd would be buried in a coffin stuffed full of wool. The explanation given for this practice was that, when the day of judgment came, Christ would see the wool, and realize that this man had been a shepherd. As Christ himself had once been a shepherd, he would know the pressures the man had faced, the amount of time needed to look after wayward sheep, and would understand why he hadn't been to church very much! Amusing though the story is, it does, however, make an important point, which we must treasure as one of the greatest of the many Christian insights into God. We are not dealing with a distant God who knows nothing of what being human, frail and mortal means. He knows and understands; and so we can 'approach the throne of grace with confidence' (Hebrews 4:16).

Who was Jesus? In this part of the book, we have been looking at questions about the identity of Jesus. But Christianity has much to say about the significance of Jesus – about what he did. We have been looking mainly at the birth and resurrection of Jesus Christ. In the next part, our attention moves away from the person of Christ as we turn to the cross, and consider the work of Christ. Why did Jesus have to die? And what are the implications for us, living some two thousand years after that event? Why is the cross universally recognized as the symbol of the Christian faith? It is to these questions that we now turn.

Part 3

The work of Jesus Christ

9

The New Testament witness to the work of Jesus

Christianity is not the religion taught or preached by Jesus. It centres on the great drama of redemption accomplished by his death and resurrection. Jesus Christ is the Saviour, someone who makes possible an entirely new life. Nor is the gospel primarily concerned with the life of a holy man or hero who serves as an example to his followers, but with a series of events in history, which are recognized as acts of divine redemption with the potential to change those who respond to them.

From the time of the New Testament onwards, the Christian church has always proclaimed the necessity, the possibility and the actuality of redemption through the death of Christ. The New Testament witness to the identity and significance of Jesus Christ culminates in his death and resurrection, rather than in his moral teaching. This is most evident in the New Testament letters, although, as we saw earlier, the same concentration on his death and resurrection may be seen as underlying the gospels as well. Jesus' death was not an accident, the untimely or premature end to the career of a promising rabbi, but something through which God was working to achieve some definite purpose.

At some point, however, we have to turn from facts to interpretations of their significance. The death and resurrection of Jesus may, as we have insisted, be regarded as historical events. But what do they mean? Why are they significant? We have already emphasized the important distinction between an event and its interpretation: there is all the difference in the world between the statements 'Jesus died' and 'Jesus died for me'. The former refers to an event, the latter to its interpretation. In this part of the book, we are going to look at interpretations of the significance of the death and resurrection of Jesus Christ, sometimes called 'theories of the atonement' (although this phrase is not particularly helpful or illuminating). The previous part dealt with the question of the person of Christ: we are now concerned with the work of Christ, an area of theology sometimes referred to as 'soteriology', from the Greek word *sotēria*, meaning 'salvation'.

New Testament images of the work of Jesus

The New Testament uses a wide range of images to express the richness of its understanding of the work of Christ. These images may be seen as analogies, models or metaphors, which allow us to explain or interpret what was going on between God, sinful humanity and Jesus Christ in the crucifixion and resurrection in terms of ideas we are already familiar with from everyday life. The New Testament writers did exactly what every good preacher is meant to do – use illustrations and analogies drawn from their experience to help 'unpack' their theology. What happened on the cross cannot be reduced to a single statement or image. It is necessary to build up a picture of what was going on by using a wide range of illustrations, each of which casts light on one particular aspect of our subject. It may well be that some people find one illustration more helpful than another. This does not, however, entitle them to argue that it is this illustration alone which is totally adequate as a description of what was going on. It will require supplementation from other images, which cast light on other aspects of the work of Christ. Let us begin by looking at seven images the New Testament uses to bring out the meaning of the death and resurrection of Jesus Christ.

Ransom

Jesus himself declared that he came 'to give his life as a ransom for many' (Mark 10:45). If Jesus originally spoke Aramaic – which seems highly likely – it is possible that we ought to translate these words as 'give his life as a ransom for all', because it is impossible to distinguish between 'many' and 'all' in Aramaic. The idea is also found elsewhere. 1 Timothy 2:5–6 speaks of Jesus Christ being a 'mediator between God and men . . . who gave his life as a ransom for all'. A ransom is a price which is paid to achieve someone's freedom. In the Old Testament, however, the emphasis falls upon the idea of being freed, of liberation, rather than speculation about the nature of the price paid, or the identity of the person to whom it is paid. Thus Isaiah 35:10 and 51:11 refer to the liberated Israelites as the 'ransomed of the Lord'. The basic idea is that God intervenes to deliver his people from captivity, whether from the power of Babylon (Isaiah 51:10–11) or of death (Hosea 13:14).

To speak of Jesus' death as a 'ransom' suggests three ideas. First, it hints at the idea of someone being held in bondage. To many readers of the New Testament, it might evoke the image of some great public figure being held captive, against his or her will. Their freedom depends totally upon someone being prepared to pay the ransom demand. This brings us to the second idea which is prompted by the image of a 'ransom' – that of a price which is paid to bring about the freedom of the captive. The more important the person being held to ransom, the greater the price demanded. One of the most astonishing things about the love of God for us is that he was prepared to pay so dearly to set us free. The price of our freedom was the death of his one and only Son (John 3:16). And thirdly, it suggests someone who is holding that person in bondage, and to whom the ransom is paid. But are all three aspects of that analogy valid? The first two certainly are; but what about the third?

The early Christian writers of the patristic era were intrigued by the question of who the ransom was paid to. Some developed the idea that Christ's death was a ransom paid to the devil, so that the satanic dominion over humanity might be broken, and we might be freed. However, as we all know only too well from experience, analogies break down very quickly! The important thing to remember when dealing with an analogy is that the crucial point which the analogy illustrates must be identified.

A similar point applies to metaphors. For example, an enthusiastic gardener might survey his magnificent display of blooming half-hardy annuals swaying in the wind, and refer to them as a 'sea of colour'. By that, he means that the observer is confronted with a vast expanse of moving colour, similar to the impression created by the sea. He does not mean that they are wet or salty! The point which he is trying to make by the analogy must be identified and appreciated!

To ask 'Who is the ransom of Jesus' life paid to?' is rather like asking 'Are the half-hardy annuals salty and wet?' We have failed to appreciate the point which is being made, and have concentrated our attention on something we weren't meant to think about at all. For the New Testament, 'ransom' means 'freedom purchased at great price'. Beyond this point the analogy breaks down. Fortunately, however, we have other analogies which we can use to explore the meaning of Christ's death. Let us go on to another, rather similar to the one we've just been looking at.

Redemption

The basic idea expressed here is that of 'buying back'. An example all too familiar from English life in the nineteenth and early twentieth century is provided by the pawnbroker. After pawning an item, it is necessary to redeem it – to buy it back from the pawnbroker, to re-establish possession of the item. A similar idea underlies the practice of redeeming slaves, a familiar event in New Testament times. A slave could redeem himself by buying his freedom. The word used to describe this event could literally be translated as 'being taken out of the forum [the slave market]'. As with the idea of ransom, we are dealing with the notion of restoring someone to a state of liberty, with the emphasis laid upon liberation, rather than upon the means used to achieve it. It is thus interesting to notice how the words 'redeemed' and 'ransomed' are used side by side at points in the Old Testament (Isaiah 55:10–11; Jeremiah 31:11; Hosea 13:14, in the Revised Standard Version).

In the Old Testament, God is often said to redeem his people (see Deuteronomy 7:8; 2 Samuel 7:23; Hosea 7:13; Zechariah 10:8). Once more, emphasis falls on the act of divine deliverance or liberation, rather than upon any money used to achieve this liberation (Isaiah 52:3 even makes it clear that money is not involved). The New Testament can use the term in the sense of being liberated from bondage – for example, bondage to the law (Galatians 3:13; 4:5). More often, however, the word is used in a more general sense – simply being set free (Revelation 5:9; 14:3–4). Here, as with the image of ransom, we are dealing with the idea of Christ's death and resurrection setting man free from his bondage to sin and death. Paul's repeated emphasis that Christians are slaves who have been 'bought at a price' (1 Corinthians 6:20; 7:23) does, however, remind us that we cannot overlook the fact that our present liberty is directly related to the death of Christ.

Justification

The idea of justification became especially important within the church at the time of the Reformation in the sixteenth century, and is used frequently by Paul. 'We are justified by faith' (Romans 5:1), and thus have peace with God. The notion of justification is based upon the idea of being 'put right', rather than being 'made righteous' or 'declared righteous'. Perhaps the English word 'rectification' expresses its meaning better. We are 'put right' with God, rather than being made morally righteous. Justification is about 'rightness' rather than 'righteousness'. When Paul speaks of 'justification by faith', he is expressing the idea that believers become right with God through faith. It may be that Paul is saying that it is faith itself which puts us right with God, or that it is through faith that we receive something which puts us right with God, or that faith is the right relationship to God. The important thing here is that we are understood to be placed in a right relationship with God through the death and resurrection of Christ (Romans 4:24–25).

There are two possible ways of drawing out the meaning of the word 'justification'. In the Old Testament, the idea often has forensic overtones – in other words, it can refer to legal proceedings. If an accused man is justified, he is declared to be in the right, or vindicated, by a judge in court. This idea can be transferred to the New Testament without difficulty. The idea that we are 'justified by the blood of Christ' (Romans 5:9) is probably best understood to mean that a sinner is vindicated by God on account of the death of Christ. The judgment that should have been pronounced upon us, on account of our sin, is transferred to Christ instead.

A second way of approaching the concept of justification is to see it as referring to a personal relationship. Justification is about the making right of the state of affairs between two parties – the establishment or re-establishment of a right relationship between God and sinful humanity, in much the same way as a right relationship might be established or re-established between two people. 'Justification by faith' could be interpreted as meaning that faith is the right relationship between believers and God. Genesis 15:6 is seen by some Old Testament scholars to mean that Abraham, by believing God, placed himself in a right relationship with him.

Salvation

This term is used frequently in the New Testament (see Acts 13:26; Ephesians 1:13; Hebrews 1:14). The verb 'to save' is generally used in the future tense, suggesting that salvation should be thought of, at least in part, as a future event – something which is still to happen in all its fullness, although it may have begun to happen in the present. The idea is that something has been inaugurated or commenced in the present, yet which will reach its fulfilment and culmination in the future. A seed has been planted and has begun to grow; its final flowering, though assured, has yet to happen. Salvation thus refers to both a present reality and a future hope. But what sort of reality and hope?

Some of the most important associations of 'salvation' are those of deliverance, preservation, or rescue, from a dangerous situation. The verb is used outside the New Testament to refer to being saved from death by the intervention of a rescuer, or to being cured from a deadly illness. The word 'salvation' is used in this sense by the Jewish historian Josephus to refer to the deliverance of the Israelites from Egyptian bondage. Earlier, we noted how the theme of deliverance is of major significance in relation to the image of 'ransom'. 'To be saved' refers to being rescued or delivered from a dangerous situation, just as the Israelites were delivered from their captivity in Egypt at the time of the Exodus. In much the same way, Christ is understood to deliver humanity from the fear of death and the penalty and power of sin. The name 'Jesus' means 'God saves'; it is clear that the New Testament understands this to mean 'saves from sin' (Matthew 1:21 should be noted here). Christ's death is the means by which the penalty due for sin is paid – a penalty which we could not hope to pay ourselves.

The biblical understanding of 'salvation' is enormously rich, and also includes the ideas of 'wholeness' or 'health'. There is a very close relation between the ideas of salvation and wholeness. In many languages, the words for 'health' and 'salvation' are one and the same. Thus it is sometimes difficult to know whether a passage should be translated in terms of salvation or wholeness. An example of this can be seen at Mark 5:34. Should the words of Jesus in this passage be translated as 'Your faith has made you whole' or 'Your faith has saved you?' The Greek word used here can bear both meanings.

This close association of ideas was also found in the English language, until the time of the Norman Conquest in 1066. The old English word for salvation (*hœl* – note the similarity to the modern English words 'heal' and 'health') was replaced by the Latin form 'salvation' at that time, so that the English-speaking world has lost this close association of both words and concepts. But in other modern languages, this close association remains. Let us explore the implications of this close relationship between 'salvation' and 'health'.

When someone who has been ill is healed, he or she is restored to their former state of health and wholeness. The creation stories of Genesis make it clear that God created humanity in a state of wholeness, and that this wholeness was lost through the Fall. Just as healing involves restoring someone to health, so salvation involves restoring believers to wholeness, to the state in which we were first created by God. Paul draws attention to the relation between the first and the second Adam (Christ): through Adam, we lost our integrity before God; through Christ, that integrity can be regained and restored.

In many ways, Christ can be thought of as having undone all that Adam did. One of the most thoughtful Christian writers of the second century, Irenaeus of Lyons, loved to draw attention to the parallels that existed between Adam and Christ. In each case, there is a parallel or symmetry between the fall through Adam and redemption through Christ. Two of the parallels that he noted, are of especial interest. First, Adam's disobedience took place in a garden (Eden); Christ's obedience took place in another garden (Gethsemane). Secondly, through Adam, the tree of life became the tree of death; through Christ, the tree of death became the tree of life. In each case, Irenaeus pointed out how the work of Christ went over the same ground as Adam, undoing the original harm done. (Irenaeus uses the term 'recapitulation' to refer to this going over again.) The restoration of humanity to spiritual health involves confronting the original cause of our sin and death, in order that these can be neutralized through Christ's obedience.

The gospel, then, is about healing. In many respects the gospel is like a medicine – something which heals us, even though we don't understand how it works. It doesn't matter that we do not fully understand exactly how God is able to work out our salvation through the death and resurrection of Christ. Christians have always believed that God could and did save us in this way, even if they couldn't quite understand how or why (although they were certainly prepared to speculate on these questions!).

Let us develop this medical analogy a little further. When I was young, I developed a bad infection which had to be treated with antibiotics. I took my penicillin, as directed by my doctor, and the infection quickly cleared up. I hadn't the slightest idea what the drug was, or how it worked. I just trusted the doctor's diagnosis, and the cure he prescribed. Many years later, as an Oxford undergraduate studying biochemistry, I learned how penicillin actually worked. As part of a course of lectures on the effects of drugs on living organisms, we were told about the way in which this antibiotic destroyed bacteria. Yet, I remember thinking at the time, it had worked perfectly well for me, even though I didn't understand exactly what was happening!

In many ways, there is an obvious parallel with the gospel proclamation of salvation in Christ, which diagnoses our problem (sin), and offers us a cure (Christ). We don't know exactly how Christ overwhelms sin (although in this part of the book we'll be looking at some suggestions), but we firmly believe, on the best authority, that he does. The theologian may fuss over the details, but the crucial thing is that Christ somehow provides a solution to the problem of the human situation. The really important thing is to know how to benefit from that solution.

'Your faith has made you whole', by restoring us to fellowship with God, and beginning the long and painful process of learning to live with God and for God. Why should it be painful? Because we have tried to live without God for so long that when we finally come to make room for him, we find it very difficult to make the adjustment. Many of us know only too well what happens when the blood circulation is restored after it has been cut off from an arm or leg. It can be acutely painful, as the limb tries to readjust to the presence of the life-giving fluid. Yet that pain comes about through the limb coming to life again. So it is with coming back to God: it is painful, but it is also coming back to life.

Reconciliation

'God was reconciling the world to himself in Christ' (2 Corinthians 5:19). This famous statement picks up the theme of 'reconciliation'. Both the word and the idea are familiar to us all. The world in which we live cries out for reconciliation between nations, groups and individuals. Paul uses the word in another context to refer to a reconciliation of an estranged husband and wife (1 Corinthians 7:11). The idea of reconciliation is fundamental to human experience, especially in the area of personal relationships. The parable of the prodigal son (Luke 15:11–32) is perhaps the supreme illustration of the importance of reconciliation in the New Testament. It illustrates vividly the reconciliation of father and son, and the restoration of their broken relationship.

The parallel between the reconciliation of two individuals on the one hand, and between God and sinners on the other will be obvious. God is treated as a person, someone to whom people can relate. Their relationship, once close (as in Eden) has been seriously disrupted, to the point where it exists in name only. We are, and will always remain, children of God. We were created by God. Sin does not destroy that relationship between the Creator and his creatures. Yet it devastates it, by robbing us of the closeness that once went with it. We read the story of Adam and Eve in the Garden of Eden with great sadness, as we realize that the closeness and intimacy of that original relationship has been forfeited through sin. It is no accident that the New Testament speaks of salvation in terms of a 'new creation' (2 Corinthians 5:17), or of the need for people to be 'born again' (John 3:1–16) if they are to see the kingdom of God.

Yet God continues to love us, despite the fact that we wander away from him, whether by accident or by deliberate choice, into the far country, away from God. It must be emphasized that the prodigal son remained the son of his father even when he set off, to live independently, confident that he could live without his father's continual presence and oversight. But that relationship exists in name only. One party to the relationship acts as if it was not there. Reconciliation takes place when both parties to a relationship take that relationship with full seriousness, and acknowledge their mutual love for each other and the obligations which they have towards each other. The son returns to his father, and they embrace – the relationship becomes real.

Reconciliation involves someone taking the initiative. If there are two persons who once enjoyed a close relationship, but now have drifted apart, that relationship will remain broken unless someone attempts a reconciliation. Someone has to take the initiative, by approaching the other party, acknowledging that the relationship has gone wrong, recalling how precious and important that relationship once was, affirming their love and concern for the other, and asking them to restore the relationship. If the other party is not prepared to restore the relationship, no progress has been made. If reconciliation is offered but not accepted, the relationship remains unaltered. There is simply no such thing as a 'legal fiction' in personal relationships! If, and only if, both parties agree to restore the relationship will reconciliation be achieved. All this is evident from our experience of everyday personal relationships. By making an appeal to personal relationships (and the parable of the prodigal son makes this appeal with remarkable power!), the New Testament grounds our relationship with God in everyday experience.

'God was in Christ reconciling the world to himself'. How is Christ understood to be involved in the reconciliation between God and sinners? There are two ways of looking at this question. First, the phrase 'God was in

Christ' can be taken as a reference to the incarnation. Christ as God incarnate makes his reconciling appeal to us. He takes the initiative in proclaiming the overwhelming love of God for us and the divine wish that we should be reconciled to him. In proclaiming the need and possibility of reconciliation to God, Christ addresses us as God and on behalf of God.

The phrase 'in Christ' can also be understood in a second way. It may reflect a Hebrew grammatical construction with which Paul would have been familiar, which would be better translated as 'through Christ'. In other words, 'God was reconciling the world to himself in Christ'. Christ is understood as the agent of divine reconciliation, the one through whom God reconciles us to him, the mediator or go-between. The following remarks from the letter to the Colossians are instructive: 'you were alienated from God . . . But now he has reconciled you by Christ's physical body through death to present you holy in his sight' (Colossians 1:21–22). The ideas of 'estrangement' (or 'alienation', as it could also be translated) and 'hostility' are used to refer to the alienated human relationship with God, which is transformed through the death of Christ into reconciliation.

A further idea associated with the reconciliation of God and sinful humanity through the death of Christ is peace. Reconciliation means the end of hostility, and the beginning of peace. Through Christ, God was pleased 'to reconcile to himself all things . . . making peace by the blood of his cross' (Colossians 1:20). Elsewhere, Paul states that one of the direct results of justification is peace with God (Romans 5:1). Christ is seen as a mediator between God and ourselves, pleading God's case to us, and our case to God. Through reconciliation, the hostility between God and humanity is abolished, and a new relationship of peace and harmony established. Christ makes an appeal to us on behalf of God, that we should be reconciled to him. Paul continues his discussion of the reconciliation of sinners to God as follows:

> God was reconciling the world to himself in Christ, not counting men's sins against them. And he has committed to us the message of reconciliation. We are therefore Christ's ambassadors, as though God were making his appeal through us (2 Corinthians 5:19–20).

The idea here is that believers are representatives of Christ in the world, just as an ambassador is the representative of a country or monarch in a foreign land.

The emphasis upon the divine initiative is important: it is God who reconciles us to him, not the other way round! God approaches us, and it is up to us to respond. It is God who takes upon himself the pain and the anguish of broaching the situation of human sin, attempting to let us know of the great distress which sin causes him, and the barrier it places between him and us. 'Your iniquities have separated you from your God', in the famous words of the prophet (Isaiah 59:1). It is God himself who discloses the full extent of his love for us, despite the fact that we are sinners. Our love of God is a result of his love for us, not the other way round: 'This is love: not that we loved God, but that he loved us and sent his Son as an atoning sacrifice for our sins' (1 John 4:10).

Adoption

The image of adoption is used by Paul to express the distinction between sons of God (believers) and the Son of God (Jesus Christ). The most important passages are Romans 8:15; 8:23; 9:4; Galatians 4:5; Ephesians 1:5. It is clear that this is an image drawn from the sphere of Roman family law, with which Paul (and many of his readers) would have been familiar. Under this law, a father was free to adopt individuals from outside his natural family, and give them a legal status of adoption, thus placing them within the family. Although a distinction would still be possible between the natural and adopted children, they have the same legal status. In the eyes of the law, they are all members of the same family, irrespective of their origins.

Paul uses this image to indicate that, through faith, believers come to have the same status as Jesus (as sons of God), without implying that they have the same divine nature as Jesus. Faith brings about a change in our status before God, incorporating us within the family of God, despite the fact that we do not share the same divine origins as Christ. Coming to faith in Christ thus brings about a change in our status. We are adopted into the family of God, with all the benefits that this brings. As the *Heidelberg Catechism* (1563) puts it, 'Christ alone is God's eternal son, whereas we are accepted for his sake as children of God by grace.'

What benefits? Two may be singled out. First, to be a member of the family of God is to be an heir of God. Paul argues this point as follows. If we are adopted as children of God, we share the same inheritance rights as the natural child. We are thus 'heirs of God' and 'co-heirs with Christ' (Romans 8:17), in that we share in the same inheritance rights as him. This means that, just as Christ suffered and was glorified, so believers may expect to do the same.

All that Christ has inherited from God will one day

be ours as well. For Paul, this insight is of considerable importance in understanding why believers undergo suffering. Christ suffered before he was glorified; believers must expect to do the same. Just as suffering for the sake of the gospel is real, so is the hope of future glory, as we will share in all that Christ has won by his obedience.

Secondly, adoption into the family of God brings a new sense of belonging. Everyone needs to feel that they belong somewhere. Social psychologists have shown the need for a 'secure base', a community or group which gives people a sense of purpose and an awareness of being valued and loved by others. In human terms, this need is usually met by the family unit. For Christians, this real psychological need is met through being adopted into the family of God. Believers can rest assured that they are valued within this family, and are thus given a sense of self-confidence which enables them to work in and witness to the world.

Forgiveness

This is perhaps the most powerful and familiar image used to explain the significance of Christ's death and resurrection. The image can be interpreted in two ways: as a legal concept, and as a personal concept. The legal use of the term is probably most familiar from the parable of the merciless servant (Matthew 18:23–35). Here forgiveness is understood in terms of the remission of a debt. The servant is heavily in debt to his master, to the extent that he cannot pay it. As an act of compassion, the master forgives him the debt. In other words, he writes it off, or cancels it. The idea of 'forgiveness of sins' may thus be regarded as a legal concept, involving the remission of obligation or penalty.

How great a theme this is! Imagine that you fall into debt. Perhaps you are overdue on a mortgage, or a credit card account. Perhaps, in desperation, you have turned to a disreputable lender who is threatening to take possession of your home and your belongings unless you repay both the loan and all the interest now due. You cannot pay. Imagine how you would feel, as you contemplate the devastating impact of this on your family, who would become homeless and helpless. Yet there is nothing that you can do about the situation. You do not have access to the funds needed to pay off the loan. For many people, that feeling corresponds more or less exactly to their sense of guilt in the presence of God. They know that they are guilty, and that they cannot do anything about it.

Now imagine the sense of utter joy and relief if someone were to offer to pay off your debt, so that you could go free. Imagine the enormous burden which would be lifted from your shoulders. That is precisely the sense of relief and delight felt by those who hear the gospel proclamation of the real forgiveness of sins through the death of Jesus Christ. The penalty due for our sin has been paid by Christ. Its guilt has been purged by his life-giving and cleansing blood. His death is the only possible and effective expiation for the guilt which the offence of human sin causes a righteous and holy God. This point is made powerfully by Mrs Cecil F. Alexander in her famous hymn *There is a Green Hill Far Away*:

> There was no other good enough
> To pay the price of sin;
> He only could unlock the gate,
> Of heaven, and let us in.

The price paid by God to achieve our forgiveness is high; his Son died in order that we might be forgiven. Yet the costliness of that forgiveness corresponds to its effectiveness. This is no cut-price deal, which promises much and delivers little. This is a forgiveness which is as real as it is costly, and is made possible and available only through the death of Jesus Christ.

The second sense of the term is probably more familiar, and is closely related to the idea of 'reconciliation'. Forgiveness is here understood as something necessary for a personal relationship to be restored to its former state after a hurtful disagreement or misunderstanding. Once more, it is necessary for the offended party to offer the other forgiveness. It again is necessary for him or her to broach a difficult and painful situation, in order to restore the relationship. If the offer of forgiveness is not accepted, the relationship remains unaltered. Forgiveness offered, yet not accepted, does not transform a relationship. As with the idea of reconciliation, we are presented with the concept of a personal, and greatly hurt God offering us his forgiveness. This is real forgiveness of real sins. The offer is real. Our acceptance of that offer must be equally real, if we are to benefit from it.

Conclusion

We have now looked at seven analogies or illustrations of what Christ achieved on the cross. Perhaps it is worth noting that they broadly fall under three categories.

1. The *commercial* or *transactional* approach. Here Christ's death is understood as the basis of a transaction, by means of which we are transferred from a state of bondage to a state of liberty. Obvious examples in this category are the ideas of ransom and redemption.

2. The *legal* approach. Here Christ's death is understood

as the means by which a change in our legal status is achieved. Examples of such an approach include being vindicated of guilt, being adopted into a family, or being forgiven a debt.

3. The *personal* approach. Here Christ's death is understood as the means by which a personal relationship between God and sinful humanity is restored, as with the images of justification (or being made 'right with God'), reconciliation and forgiveness.

It would be possible to extend this list considerably, and give an exhaustive list of ideas, analogies or metaphors used to explain what it was that Christ achieved on the cross. This exercise would probably be interesting, but is not particularly relevant to our purposes. In the following three chapters, we will look at three main 'theories of the atonement' – ways of making sense of the significance of the death of Christ – which have been influential over the last two thousand years of Christian history.

The phrase 'theories of the atonement' needs a little explanation. The term 'the atonement' is a kind of theological shorthand for 'all that Jesus Christ achieved for us on the cross'. It owes its origins to the English reformer William Tyndale (1494–1536), who introduced it in his English translation of the New Testament to translate the Greek word for 'reconciliation'. The term caught on, and has since been used extensively to refer to the general benefits which result to believers on account of Christ's death and resurrection. The phrase 'theories of the atonement' refers to ways of explaining how these specific benefits arise from the work of Christ. These theories are attempts to develop insights contained in the New Testament in a more systematic manner. We will begin by focusing on approaches to the atonement which place a particular emphasis upon the victory of God over forces which oppress his people.

10

The victorious God

The theme of God's victory over hostile forces is often encountered in the Old Testament. Creation itself is often regarded as a divine victory over the forces of chaos (see Job 26:12–13; Psalm 89:9–10). This great theme of God's victory over sin, evil and oppression is, of course, most obvious in the Old Testament accounts of the exodus from Egypt. God is seen as having delivered his people from their captivity, and having gained a historic victory over the forces of oppression and darkness, which would culminate with the entry of Israel into the promised land of Canaan. The great triumph song of Exodus 15 exults in this victory:

> I will sing to the Lord, for he is highly exalted. The horse and its rider he has hurled into the sea. The Lord is my strength and my song; he has become my salvation. (Exodus 15:1–2).

It was through this act of divine deliverance that Israel was brought into existence as a people, and Israel never forgot its importance. Time and time again the Psalms recall that great act and look forward to similar divine victories in the future (see Psalms 135 and 136).

If the Exodus from Egypt is viewed by the Old

Testament as a divine victory marking one turning point in the history of Israel, the return from exile in Babylon is viewed as the second. In the sixth century BC, the city of Jerusalem was besieged and captured by the Babylonians, and many of its inhabitants were deported to a life of exile in the city of Babylon. It is this long period of exile which lies behind the deep sense of nostalgia found in the following words:

> By the rivers of Babylon we sat and wept when we remembered Zion. There on the poplars we hung our harps, for there our captors asked us for songs, our tormentors demanded songs of joy; they said, 'Sing us one of the songs of Zion!' How can we sing the songs of the Lord while in a foreign land? (Psalm 137:1–4).

That captivity lasted half a century, and some of the exiles seem to have given up hope of ever seeing Jerusalem again. As the captivity wore on, a new prophet arose among the exiled people, who proclaimed that God would soon deliver his people from Babylon, just as he had once delivered them from Egypt (Isaiah 40 – 55). In a great moment of vision, the prophet sees God acting decisively to redeem his people:

> Awake, awake! Clothe yourself with strength, O arm of the Lord; awake, as in days gone by, as in generations of old. Was it not you who cut Rahab to pieces, who pierced that monster through? Was it not you who dried up the sea, the waters of the great deep, who made a road in the depths of the sea so that the redeemed might cross over? The ransomed of the Lord will

return. They will enter Zion with singing; everlasting joy will crown their heads. (Isaiah 51:9–11).

The theme of the 'Lord laying bare his holy arm before the nations' (Isaiah 52:9–10), which runs throughout this great prophecy, is a theme of divine victory and divine deliverance. It is this vision of the great and mighty acts of God in history, by which his people are delivered and preserved, which is summed up in one of the most famous passages in this prophecy:

How beautiful on the mountains are the feet of those who bring good news, who proclaim peace, who bring good tidings, who proclaim salvation, who say to Zion, 'Your God reigns!' Listen! Your watchmen lift up their voices; together they shout for joy. When the Lord returns to Zion, they will see it with their own eyes. Burst into songs of joy together, you ruins of Jerusalem, for the Lord has comforted his people, he has redeemed Jerusalem. (Isaiah (52:7–9).

This theme of the victory of God in delivering his people from captivity became deeply embedded in the hopes and expectations of Israel as the centuries passed. Israel once more came to be under foreign rule, first occupied by the Greeks, then by the Romans. But the great theme of deliverance continued to be celebrated by Jews in the festival of Passover. By recalling the way in which God had rescued them from their hardship and bondage in Egypt, they were given hope that the same God would rescue them once more in the future.

Passover and the cross

The Jewish feast of Passover celebrates the events leading up to the exodus and the establishment of the people of Israel. The passover lamb, slaughtered shortly before, and eaten at the feast, symbolizes this great act of divine redemption. It is thus very significant that the last supper and the crucifixion of Jesus took place at the feast of Passover. The Synoptic Gospels clearly treat the last supper as a Passover meal, with Jesus initiating a new version of the meal. While Jews celebrated their deliverance by God from Egypt by eating a lamb, Christians would henceforth celebrate their deliverance by God from sin by eating bread and drinking wine. Passover celebrates the great act of God by which the people of Israel came into being; the Lord's Supper celebrates the great saving act of God by which the Christian church came into being, and to which she owes her life and her existence.

John's gospel suggests that Jesus is crucified at exactly the same moment as the slaughter of the passover lambs, indicating even more forcefully that Jesus is the true passover lamb, who died for the sins of the world. The real passover lamb is not being slaughtered in the temple precincts, but on the cross. In the light of this, the full meaning of the words of John the Baptist can be appreciated: 'Behold the Lamb of God, who takes away the sin of the world' (John 1:29). The death of Christ takes away our sins, and cleanses us from its guilt and stain.

The coincidence of the last supper and the crucifixion with the Passover feast makes it clear that there is a vitally close connection between the exodus and the death of Christ. Both are to be seen as acts of divine deliverance from oppression. However, while Moses led

Israel from a specific captivity in Egypt, Christ is seen as delivering his people from a universal bondage to sin and death. While there are parallels between the exodus and the cross; there are also differences. Perhaps the most important difference relates to the universality of the redemption accomplished by Christ. As the New Testament makes clear, the work of Christ benefits all who put their trust in him, irrespective of their historical or geographical location. The universal human predicament of sin and death is met by a universal saving response, by which God delivers us from the presence, power and penalty of sin and the fear of death, on account of Christ's saving death upon the cross. We who ought to die for our sin go free; Christ dies in our place.

This idea is developed most fully in the New Testament letters, especially those of Paul. The death and resurrection of Christ are often reaffirmed as a decisive act of divine deliverance, by which we have been liberated from the tyranny of sin and death. Paul draws on images of conflict taken from the battlefield, the amphitheatre and the athletic stadium to bring out the full significance of this theme of victory. 'Thanks be to God who has given us the victory through our Lord Jesus Christ' (1 Corinthians 15:57). For the writers of the New Testament, the forces of evil are as real as the forces of good. Despite the fact that they have little to say to explain its origins, they never attempt to explain it away. For Paul, God 'disarmed the principalities and powers, and made a public example of them, triumphing over them in him [Christ]' (Colossians 2:15).

In John's gospel, we also find the cross interpreted as a symbol of victory – victory over darkness, death and the world (John 12.31–33 is particularly important here). Thus the final words of Jesus from the cross – 'It is finished' (John 19:30) – should not be seen as a cry of hopeless defeat, meaning 'It is all over'. Rather, those words should be seen as a shout of triumph and exultation: 'It is accomplished!'. What needed to be done was done, and was done well.

The cross as God's victory

The idea of God's victory over the forces of sin, death and evil in the cross has always had enormous dramatic power, making a powerful appeal to the human imagination. The New Testament writers are content to indicate that, somehow, God achieved a great victory through the death of Christ, and that this victory affects believers here and now. But Christianity soon exploded into the first century mediterranean world, and Christian preachers found that this way of looking at the death of Christ seemed to lack something. It did not explain why Christ had to die, or how this victory was specifically related to the cross. Later writers therefore developed this idea along lines somewhat different to those found in the New Testament. An illustration from the works of the sixth-century writer Gregory the Great will make this clear.

According to Gregory, the devil had managed to gain rights over sinful humanity, on account of sin, and God was not in a position to violate those rights in order to deliver us from the power of the devil. Therefore God devised a cunning plan by which the devil might be trapped. God sent into the world someone who looked like a sinful human being, but who was actually sinless, Jesus Christ. The devil, not realizing that Jesus was sinless, naturally assumed that he could claim his rights over him, and eventually took his life. Gregory likens what happened next to a great fish being caught on a baited fish-hook. The devil saw only the bait (Christ's humanity) and not the hook (Christ's divinity), and so found himself trapped. Having overstepped his authority, the devil's rights over sinful humanity were forfeit, and God was thus able to deliver us from the power of the devil. Other writers suggested that the cross was more like a mousetrap than a fish-hook, but the same basic ideas were still used. It need hardly be added that the New Testament was quite innocent of this type of speculation!

Another way of approaching the New Testament's emphasis upon victory over sin and death through Christ may be found in a famous eleventh century Easter hymn by Fulbert, bishop of Chartres:

> For Judah's Lion bursts his chains
> Crushing the serpent's head;
> And cries aloud through death's domain,
> To wake the imprisoned dead.

This highly imaginative hymn takes up the image of Jesus Christ as the conquering lion of the tribe of Judah, developed in the book of Revelation (Revelation 5:5), who fulfils the great promise of redemption made to Adam, by which he will trample the serpent under his feet (Genesis 3:15). The tyranny of death over sinful humanity is broken by Christ's death and resurrection. It is interesting to note that Christ uses death to defeat death, a point often made by medieval preachers. An appeal was often made to the story of David and Goliath: just as David killed Goliath with the giant's own sword, so Christ defeated death with its own weapons.

The idea of Christ 'wakening the imprisoned dead' reflects the belief that Christ's death and resurrection were important, not only for those alive at the time and in years to come, but for those who had come before. The basic idea is that Christ's victory over death is retrospective as well as prospective, to lapse into theological jargon for a moment, and is thus good news for those who have already died. These are understood to be prisoners held captive by death, and through the defeat of death by Christ, they are delivered from their bondage, and free.

In the Middle Ages, this theme would be developed as the 'Harrowing of Hell', an idea based loosely upon some New Testament passages which could be interpreted as suggesting that Christ went down to the place of the dead – in other words, Hell – between his crucifixion and resurrection (Matthew 12:39–40; Acts 2:27–31; Romans 10:7; Colossians 1:18, and especially 1 Peter 3:18–22). The basic idea is that Christ descended to Hell, with the cross of victory, took the castle of Hell by storm, setting free all those held prisoner. In the great portrayals of this scene dating from the fourteenth century, Christ tends to appear like a medieval knight, using his cross as a lance to break down the castle doors.

Perhaps the most well known portrayal of this powerful image familiar to modern readers is found in that most remarkable of religious allegories – C. S. Lewis' *The Lion, The Witch and the Wardrobe* . The book tells the story of Narnia, a land which is discovered by accident by four children rummaging around in an old wardrobe. In this work, we encounter the White Witch, who keeps the land of Narnia covered in wintry snow. As we read on, we realize that she rules Narnia not as a matter of right, but by stealth. The true ruler of the land is absent; in his absence, the witch subjects the land to oppression. In the midst of this land of winter stands the witch's castle, within which many of the inhabitants of Narnia have been imprisoned as stone statues.

As the narrative moves on, we discover that the rightful ruler of the land is Aslan, a lion. As Aslan advances into Narnia, winter gives way to spring, and the snow begins to melt. The witch realizes that her power is beginning to fade. In the fourteenth chapter of the book, Lewis describes the killing of Aslan, perhaps the most demonic episode ever to have found its way into a children's story. The forces of darkness and oppression seem to have won a terrible victory – and yet, in that victory lies their defeat. Aslan surrenders himself to the forces of evil, and allows them to do their worst with him – and by so doing, disarms them. In the famous words of William Cullen Bryant, 'Truth crushed to earth will rise again'.

Lewis' description of the resurrection of Aslan is one of his more tender moments, evoking the deep sense of sorrow so evident in the New Testament accounts of the burial of Christ, and the joy of recognition of the reality of the resurrection. In the sixteenth chapter of the book, Lewis graphically describes how Aslan – the lion of Judah, who has burst his chains – breaks into the castle, breathes upon the statues, and restores them to life, before leading the liberated army through the shattered gates of the once great fortress to freedom. Hell has been harrowed. It has been despoiled, and its inhabitants liberated from its dreary shades.

Assurance of victory amid continuing struggle

The struggle between good and evil continues to this day. So how can we talk about the cross as a decisive victory over evil? The crucifixion and resurrection are seen by the New Testament writers as a turning point, a decisive battle in God's war against the evil powers that enslave and incapacitate us. This war was not begun with the birth of Christ, nor was it ended with his resurrection. The struggle has been going on since the beginning of time, and continues to this day. But the death and resurrection of Christ mark the dawn of a new and decisive phase in this struggle, in which victory has been gained, and yet not gained. To illustrate this point, let us consider a modern example, drawn from the Second World War (1939–45).

On a fateful day in June 1944, Allied forces managed to establish a bridgehead in Nazi-occupied Europe, on the beaches of Normandy. This momentous day was called D-Day, and historians have emphasized that it marked a decisive turning point in the history of the Second World War. The war was not won on that day; in fact, victory did not come until the following year, on VE-Day. But, in a sense, the war was won on that day, because from that moment onwards, the war entered a new phase, a phase of victory. Looking back on the history of the Second World War, the great turning point in that history may be identified as that seizing of a bridgehead, a small pocket of Allied land in the midst of hostile territory, in June 1944.

So it is with the incarnation, death and resurrection of Jesus Christ. In the incarnation, God established a bridgehead in hostile territory from which to begin the reconquest of his own world. In Christ's death and resurrection, we see the age-old conflict between good and evil entering a new phase. It has not yet been won, but it is as if we have been granted a preview of the end of history, and can know that, in the end, evil will be destroyed. From that standpoint, the cross and resurrection are seen as the turning point, the moment in which victory was gained, and yet not gained. The cross and resurrection are to D-Day as the end of history is to VE-Day. We know that sin and death are defeated, even if the battle goes on around us.

The price of victory

Does not the emphasis upon the victory given in the cross diminish the place of the suffering of Christ in obtaining this victory? This is a real danger; however, it is easily avoided. One of the most powerful pieces of reflection upon the meaning of the cross was written before 750 in Old English, and is widely known as the *Dream of the Rood* ('Rood' is the Old English, or Anglo-Saxon, word for 'cross'). In this poem, the writer tells of how he dreamed 'the best of dreams', in which he saw a cross studded with the jewels and richness of victory:

> It was as though I saw a wondrous tree
> Towering in the sky, diffused with light.

Yet, as he wonders at this 'glorious tree of victory', it changes its appearance before his eyes, appearing to become covered with blood and gore. How can this be, that this strange tree should have two so very different appearances? As he wonders, the cross begins to speak for itself, telling him its story. It tells of how it was once a young tree, growing in a forest, only to be chopped down, and taken to a hill. When it had been firmly put in its place, a hero came, and voluntarily mounted it:

> Then the young hero (who was God almighty)
> Got ready, resolute, and strong in heart.
> He climbed onto the lofty gallows-tree,

Bold in the sight of all who watched,
For he intended to redeem us all.

As the tree watches in horror, the young hero is pierced
with dark nails. The tree is penetrated by these same
nails, and soaked with the blood which pours from the
hero's wounds. Yet through this appalling suffering
victory is gained, and we are set free. The poet tries to
show how the glorious cross of victory (perhaps an
allusion to the jewelled crosses carried in processions in
churches at the time) was once pierced with nails and
drenched with blood. The price of glory is suffering and
death. This is no cheap victory, but a costly and precious
undertaking. Through the suffering of Christ on the
'gallows tree', the love of God for us was demonstrated,
and the bonds of sin snapped.

May God be friend to me
He who suffered once upon the gallows tree
Here on earth for our sins. He redeemed us
And granted us our life and heavenly home.

If this seems to amount to triumphalism, it must be
remembered that the victory won is not that of force, but
of tenderness. The book of Revelation gives us a symbol
of Christ's victory over all our opponents. What is that
symbol? A mighty conquering hero, on a superbly
equipped battle horse, representing a victory of sheer
naked power? No. It is a slaughtered lamb (Revelation
5:12), a symbol which mixes tenderness and death, and
points to the sacrifice of Christ as the Lamb of God, who
takes away the sin of the world. God's victory over sin
and death is won through the tender and loving obedience of Christ.

Why is this theme of the divine victory over sin, death and evil so important? Perhaps the most convincing answer to this question is given by the civil rights advocate Martin Luther King (1929–68) in his famous sermon 'The death of evil upon the seashore'. (The title of the sermon reflects a phrase in Exodus 14:30, 'Israel saw the Egyptians lying dead on the shore'.) The belief that God has already entered into battle with the forces of evil gives hope to us as we attempt to wrestle with evil in our own day. As we struggle to defeat the forces of evil, we know that God is struggling with us. At the very moment when evil seems to gain its greatest victory, it is defeated with its own weapons. The faith that God has entered into our conflict against our enemies, on our side, sustains us in our struggle to escape from the bondage of every evil. The great theme of 'the victorious God' gives hope where otherwise there would be despair, and sustains us in our endless, and seemingly unwinnable, fight against evil. The darkness and despair of Good Friday must give way to the triumph of Easter Day. As Martin Luther King so wisely observed, 'without such faith, our highest dreams will pass silently to the dust'.

The theme of victory, then, is a major component of the 'word of the cross'. It offers us hope – not some spurious hope, based upon a naive and make-believe trust that one day all will be well, but a hope which is securely grounded in the bedrock of the death and resurrection of Jesus Christ. It reassures us that, although we continue to experience the power of sin and the reality of death, their power has nonetheless been broken. In view of the importance of the theme of the breaking of the power of sin, we now turn to explore the way in which the death of Christ relates to forgiveness.

11

The forgiving God

The great theme of a loving God who forgives his wayward people is touchingly portrayed in the parable of the prodigal son (Luke 15:11–32). The waiting father, as we shall see, rushes out to greet the returning son, and forgive him for his waywardness. The parable draws our attention to the love of the father for his son. It also raises a question for many people: how can the father just forgive the son like that? It seems rather superficial, almost as if the father is suggesting that the past may be forgotten, set aside as if it never happened. Our sympathies actually often lie with the second son, who is outraged by the father's behaviour!

It is, however, unfair to expect a single parable to bring out the many aspects of the Christian understanding of the nature of forgiveness, and dispense with the remainder of the New Testament. This parable focuses our attention upon the love of the father. Parables often just make one point, and the point which this particular parable makes is that a loving God eagerly awaits the return of his wayward children. This is one aspect of the Christian understanding of God; it would be quite ridiculous to suppose that this is all that there is to it! It is an insight which is to be treasured, but it is by no means all that has to be said about God's relations with us. There are many passages in the New Testament which draw attention to the seriousness with which God takes sin, and the great cost of true forgiveness. The Lord's Prayer draws a direct comparison between God's forgiveness of our sins, and our forgiveness of other people's sins (Matthew 6:12; 14–15), and makes it clear that if we don't forgive the sins of others, God won't forgive ours.

The cost of true forgiveness

Most people know from their own experience, only too painfully, how very difficult it is to forgive someone. It is easy to forgive someone for something unimportant – but when it is something which means a lot to us, we find it very difficult. It is here that the difference between real and false forgiveness becomes clear. It is relatively easy to say 'I forgive you' to someone who has deeply hurt us, and not mean it. Resentment against that person remains, and we have 'forgiven' them in word only, and not in reality. Real forgiveness means confronting the hurt and offence which has been caused, recognizing its full extent and importance. It means going to the person who has caused such hurt and pain, and explaining the situation to him or her. It means explaining that, despite the great hurt and injury which has been done, their continued friendship is of such importance that you want them to accept your offer of forgiveness.

That is a difficult offer for someone to accept. It involves a deeply humbling admission, that offence has been given and injury has been caused. None of us likes to admit that kind of thing. It may even be that we are unaware of the hurt and pain we cause by our actions to those whom we love. Forgiveness is an essential aspect of human personal relationships. Without real forgiveness, our relationships with others would be false and superficial.

It is the same with our relationship with God. The cross brings home to us the deep hurt, offence and pain which our sin causes to God. God is angered by our sin; in Christ, he makes clear how painful and costly true forgiveness really is by demonstrating how serious sin is in the first place. The offer of forgiveness of our sins is both deeply humiliating and deeply satisfying. It is humiliating, because it forces us to recognize and acknowledge our sin; it is satisfying, because the very offer of forgiveness implies that God treats us as being important to him. God offers us a real forgiveness in Christ which, if accepted, will transform our relationship with him. God offers us forgiveness because, despite our sin, he loves us and wants us to return to him, to relate to him as we are meant to. God created us in his image and likeness (Genesis 1:26–27): there is an inbuilt capacity to relate to God within us which sin threatens to frustrate, and which forgiveness offers to restore.

The theme of the 'image of God in humanity' is an important one, and worth thinking about a little more. When I was at school, we used to enjoy playing around with chemicals in the school laboratory. One of the more amusing tricks was to get a really old copper coin, and drop it in a beaker of dilute nitric acid. The acid would turn blue, and rather unpleasant brown fumes would be given off. As these fumes dispersed, the coin would appear as new. The acid had dissolved the dirt and grime which had obscured the features of the coin. The coins that we used for this experiment were old British pennies, which had the image of Queen Victoria stamped upon them. This image was quite invisible, on account of the accumulated layers of dirt. Although the image was there, it could not be seen. By getting rid of this accumulated debris, the acid restored the image so that it was clearly and brilliantly visible.

Christianity has always insisted that although the image of God in humanity is obscured and hidden through sin, it remains there nevertheless. It just needs something to restore it (a theological equivalent of dilute nitric acid). The gospel could be seen as restoring the image of God, our ability to relate to God, by removing the obstacles to this relationship. Forgiveness does not mean that sin is eliminated from our lives, but that the threat which sin poses to our relationship to God has been eliminated. There is all the difference in the world between being sinless and being forgiven!

So far, however, we have just been talking about personal relationships. What about the wider consequences of forgiveness? What about its effect upon a group of people, upon the community? The distinction that we are moving towards drawing is well known, and in English law is summed up in the difference between a tort and a crime. A tort is a personal injury, something which somebody does to me (like being rude to me in the absence of witnesses) which has no effect on anyone but me, and which I can forgive without involving anyone else. A crime is something which someone does to me (like robbing me, or murdering me) which has wider effects upon the community. Robbing and murdering injure the community as a whole, and not just me as an individual. As a result, these actions have to be dealt with by the community. If anyone can be said to 'forgive' these actions, it is the community against which they have been committed, and not just me as an individual.

It is here that we are forced to recognize that human

sin has consequences not just for the relationship of an individual with God, but for the relationship of people in general. This is particularly clear in the Old Testament, where the destructive effects of sin upon the community of Israel are emphasized. Sin is about self-centredness, which means that we ignore both God and our neighbour in our actions. The impact of sin is felt at both the private and the communal level. The question of how God can forgive sin concerns the justice of this forgiveness. How can God forgive sin, when it has such consequences for society? Will this forgiveness not encourage us to commit sin?

God forgives sin through Christ

The New Testament emphasizes that Christ had to die in order for our sin to be forgiven. But in what way can his death procure our forgiveness? Legal approaches to the atonement answer this question by demonstrating that God acts completely justly in forgiving sin through the death of Christ. Although the roots of this idea are deeply embedded in both the Old and New Testaments, the first systematic development of the theory is to be found in the works of Anselm, an eleventh-century Archbishop of Canterbury.

Anselm expresses his dissatisfaction with the existing understanding of the death of Christ as a victory over sin, death and evil, because it does not really explain why Christ is involved in this victory in the first place. While not disputing that Christ's death and resurrection do represent a victory over sin and death, Anselm feels that too many questions are left unanswered. Why could God not have gained this great victory in some other way? How does Christ's death come into the picture? Anselm therefore sets out to develop a theory which

211

firmly establishes the necessity of the death of Christ as the means by which God worked out the salvation of the world.

His argument goes like this. God created humanity in order that we might have eternal life. Unfortunately, sin intervened to make it impossible for us to gain eternal life unaided. If we are to have eternal life, God will have to do something about it. God cannot just pretend that sin doesn't exist, or dismiss it as unimportant. It is a force which threatens to disrupt all that God intends for his creation. A remedy must be found for sin, which undoes its effects yet takes its moral aspects seriously. Anselm stresses that sin is a moral problem. It cannot just be ignored; it must be confronted and dealt with. So how can the offence of sin be purged? How can sin be forgiven justly, in a way that both acknowledges the offence caused to God by sin and his loving-kindness?

In answering these questions, Anselm draws an analogy from the feudal outlook of the period. In ordinary life, an offence against a person can be forgiven, provided that some sort of compensation is given for the offence. Anselm refers to this compensation as a 'satisfaction'. For example, a man might steal a sum of money from his neighbour. In order to meet the demands of justice, the man would have to restore that sum of money, plus an additional sum for the offence given by the theft in the first place. It is this additional sum of money which is the 'satisfaction' in question. Anselm then argues that sin is a serious offence against God, for which a satisfaction is required. As God is infinite, this satisfaction must also be infinite. But as we are finite, we cannot pay this satisfaction. So it seems impossible that we shall ever have eternal life.

Anselm then makes the following point. Although we, as sinful human beings, ought to pay the satisfaction, we cannot. On the other hand, although God is under no obligation to pay the satisfaction, he clearly could do so if he wanted to. So, Anselm argues, it is quite clear that a God-man would be both able and obliged to pay this satisfaction. Therefore the incarnation and death of Jesus Christ may be seen as a means of resolving this dilemma. As a human being, Christ has an obligation to pay the satisfaction; as God, he has the ability to pay it. The satisfaction is thus paid off, and we are enabled to regain eternal life.

Anselm's theory was important, because it showed that a good case could be made for involving the death of Christ in the scheme of the divine forgiveness of sin, without contravening justice. The theory has, of course, been very heavily criticized. For example, Anselm makes use of feudal ideas, drawn from the early Middle Ages in Europe, to make some of his points. But Anselm was just doing what every good preacher tries to do: he used contemporary analogies to make a theological point! In a feudal society, you use feudal analogies! We can hardly expect him to have imagined what life would be like in the sixteenth or twentieth centuries!

The basic point which Anselm made is still of crucial importance: God does not act in an arbitrary or unjust way in redeeming sinful humanity, but is totally faithful to his righteousness. God is not involved in questionable actions (like deceiving the devil) nor does he pretend that sin is something insignificant which can be overlooked. For Anselm, God is just, and acts in accordance with that justice in redeeming us. It is this authentic New Testament insight which Anselm so vigorously upheld, even if his defence of the insight took him far from the more cautious statements of the New Testament on the matter.

A useful distinction which may be made here is between 'justice' or 'law', and 'laws'. The terms 'law' or 'justice' express the basic principle of not acting arbitrarily, but in accordance with generally accepted standards. On the other hand, 'laws' are various expressions of what those standards might be. Thus practically everyone agrees that 'law' is a good thing, but when it comes to defining what it means, disagreement arises. 'Law' is recognized as essential, while the 'laws' which express it are a matter for debate. Anselm justifies the idea of redemption by law by an appeal to eleventh-century laws, just as Calvin made an appeal to sixteenth-century laws. The fact that those laws no longer apply today does not, however, invalidate the basic principle he is trying to establish. The legal approach to the death of Christ is concerned with law, rather than with laws – in other words, with the basic conviction that God acts justly in dealing with sin and redeeming mankind. The cross demonstrates that the guilt of sin is really forgiven, and makes clear the full cost of this forgiveness.

The New Testament itself is not particularly concerned with the mechanics of the death of Christ. There is relatively little discussion of the question of how it is that God is able to forgive our sins through the death of Christ. By drawing analogies with the Old Testament sacrificial system, and the 'Suffering Servant' of Isaiah 53, the New Testament gives us hints about ways in which we might relate Christ's death to our forgiveness, and these hints have been developed in the various legal theories of the atonement. All these theories make the same point made so simply by Fanny J. Crosby, in her hymn *To God be the Glory!*

To God be the glory! Great things he hath done!
So loved he the world that he gave us his Son,
Who yielded his life an atonement for sin,
And opened the life-gate that all may go in.

The New Testament's real concern lies elsewhere – in the emphatic assertion and proclamation that God has dealt justly with our sin, through the cross of Christ. It was through the cross alone that real forgiveness of real sins became possible. How this was done is a question of interest; nevertheless, this question is actually of little importance in comparison with the fact that it was done. The guilt and power of sin were broken through Christ.

The New Testament prefers to exult in the joy of forgiveness and eternal life and declare what needs to be done to benefit from Christ's death, rather than go into precise theoretical detail concerning how Christ made forgiveness possible. Nevertheless, anyone wishing to develop such a theory will find that Scripture has laid a thorough foundation for them. However, it is important to appreciate that theories which are based on Scripture do not have the same status as Scripture itself. It is always necessary to make sure that any resulting 'theory of the atonement' does not become detached from its biblical foundations. Anselm's approach, for instance, hardly makes reference to the New Testament at all!

The New Testament makes it clear that sin is a very serious matter. Yet modern western culture has a tendency to trivialize sin, treating it as something of minor importance. The fact that Christ had to die to secure forgiveness of sin ought to remind us that this is unacceptable. Sin causes God offence, and justly provokes his righteous anger. This point is made well by the *Heidelberg Catechism* (1563):

Throughout [Christ's] life on earth, but especially at the end of it, he bore in body and soul the wrath of God against the sin of the whole human race, so that by his suffering, as the only expiatory sacrifice, he might redeem our body and soul from everlasting damnation, and might obtain for us God's grace, righteousness and eternal life.

Yet this does not mean that the New Testament portrays God as a tyrant who arbitrarily demands the suffering and death of an innocent victim, in order that the guilty party may escape his anger. The idea of a bloodthirsty, vengeful God has no place in the New Testament, which affirms that God himself entered into history in order to suffer for offending sinners. God is the one who has been hurt by the offence of our sin; yet it is that same God who, in love, chose to suffer so that the guilt of sin might be cancelled. If anyone suffers, it is God himself on our behalf and in our place, in order that justice and mercy might both be satisfied. It is the judge himself who suffers in order that his own law may be upheld, and that we might be truly and justly forgiven.

Forgiveness, if it is to be real forgiveness, is a costly business. Just how much it costs God to forgive our sin is shown in the cross. The torment of the dying Christ, the incarnate God, gives us a most vivid and distressing insight into the nature and extent of God's forgiving love. As the 'Dream of the Rood' puts it so powerfully:

This is the tree of glory
On which God Almighty once suffered torment
For the many sins of humanity and for the deeds
Of Adam long ago.

It is God who suffers, in order to bring home to us how precious a thing real forgiveness can be. Although forgiveness is a difficult offer to accept, because of the clear implication that we are at fault, the thought of the crucified God makes this an offer we may find easier to accept than might otherwise be the case.

The love and compassion shown in God's forgiveness make the gentle chiding of our faithlessness more bearable. Christ is the only person in history to see sin through the eyes of God, to see sin for what it really is. In the crucifixion we are shown the full horror of the consequences of sin, and the urgency of the call to repent, to turn away from it to the one who alone may break its hold upon us. The cross reveals both the seriousness of sin, and the purpose and power of God to overcome it.

How, then, are we involved in this process of forgiveness? Three main ways of understanding this may be discerned in the New Testament. The first is that of *substitution* – Christ, the righteous one, takes our place on the cross. It is we who should have been crucified, yet Christ took our place, removing from us the penalties due for sin. This idea is suggested by several passages in the New Testament. 'God made him who had no sin to be sin for us, so that in him we might become the righteousness of God' (2 Corinthians 5:21). The image here is that of Christ taking our burden of sin upon himself, in order that we might become righteous in the sight of God.

The second way is *participation* – believers participate in the forgiveness which Christ won upon the cross. This view draws upon many New Testament passages, particularly Romans 8:12–30, in which the involvement of the believer with all that Christ has done is constantly emphasized. We share in Christ's suffering, death, and final glorification.

The third approach is that of *representation* – Christ represents us to God, just as he represents God to us. As our representative, Christ wins forgiveness for us on our behalf. He is thus understood to suffer on the cross on behalf of, but not necessarily instead of, sinful humanity.

Whichever of these models the reader finds most helpful in dealing with the New Testament statements on the involvement of the believer in the death and resurrection of Christ, the fact that we are involved in some way is not questioned. In some way, each of us may be said to have been present at Christ's crucifixion, just as each of us may be said to share in his resurrection.

Why is the idea of forgiveness so important? We need to know that, despite the seriousness of our sin, we may enter into fellowship with God. One of the most remarkable features of the gospel is the assertion that we are brought to God through God being brought to us. There are many religions which teach that God does not welcome us until we cease being sinners, declaring that we must become righteous before we can enter into fellowship with God.

Christianity has something more radical and liberating to declare. God loves sinners! God in Christ first welcomes us, and in that way brings about a real transformation within us. Forgiveness imparts, rather than demands, newness of life. 'We must learn to accept that we have been accepted, despite being unacceptable' (Paul Tillich). It is the offer of forgiveness, so powerfully and tenderly embodied in the dying Son of God, Jesus Christ, which brings home to us the necessity of repentance and amendment. We can come to God, just as we are, knowing that the offer of pardon and forgiveness carries with it the promise of transformation and renewal. The opening words of the well known hymn by Charlotte Elliot state this point perfectly:

> Just as I am, without one plea
> But that thy blood was shed for me,
> And that thou bidst me come to thee,
> O Lamb of God, I come.

12

The loving God

The death of Jesus Christ demonstrates the overwhelming love of God for sinners. Perhaps the most famous statement of the extent of this love may be found in John's gospel: 'God so loved the world that he gave his only son, that whoever believes in him should not perish, but have everlasting life' (John 3:16). But how does the death of Christ demonstrate this love of God for us? To answer this question, we must go back to the theme of the love of God in the Old Testament.

The love of God for his people

The theme of the love of God for his people is deeply embedded in both the Old and the New Testaments. One of the great themes expounded by the Old Testament prophets is the love of God for Israel, which he demonstrated by delivering her from bondage in Egypt and leading her into the promised land. God did not love his people on account of their greatness, achievements or numerical strength; he loved them in much the same way as a father loves his children (Deuteronomy 7:7–9). The eighth-century prophets in particular portray God reflecting with sadness on the way the child whom he loved so dearly has wandered away from him. One of the most powerful statements of this theme is found in the prophet Hosea, who portrays God as a father who loves his child, and patiently teaches him to walk, only to discover that the child decides to walk out of his life (Hosea 11:1–4). Israel is depicted as the wayward child of God, who God brought into being, cared for and supported while still incapable of looking after herself, and finally being led into the promised land. God is also likened to a mother, who can never forget the child to whom she gave birth. In the same way, God can never forget his people (Isaiah 49:14–15). Even though Israel abandons and rejects her God, God continues to love her (Hosea 14:4).

God is frequently portrayed as musing over the delight he will feel when Israel returns to him, to dwell under his protection (for example, see Hosea 14:4–7). The great covenant formula, 'You will be my people, and I will be your God', is seen as establishing a relationship between God and his people, which nothing can destroy. It may be threatened by the great empires of the world, or by the disobedience of Israel herself, yet God, in his love, remains faithful to his people.

This theme is taken up and developed in the New Testament, perhaps most powerfully in the parable of the prodigal son (Luke 15:11–32). The story is well known; perhaps our familiarity with it has blinded us to its full impact. It tells of a father and his son, and invites us to imagine a close relationship between them, which is ruptured when the son decides to assert his independence and leave home. The son then goes off into a far country, leaving his father behind as little more than a memory. Yet life apart from his father turns out not to be as rosy as he had expected. He falls on hard times.

In this parable, we may see the story of a generation

in our own times. In the 1960s and 1970s, many chose to abandon any kind of faith in God, and go their own way. It was seen as a radical and acceptable thing to do. Who needed God? So a generation of young people went off into a 'far country'. Then they discovered that life there wasn't so good after all. Like the prodigal son, they begin to think something that once would have been unthinkable: let's go home again. The parable of the prodigal son affirms that there is a home to return to, and that God is waiting with open arms, to receive those who come home.

The prodigal son comes to long to return home to his father. He is convinced that his father will have dis-owned him and will no longer wish to acknowledge him as his son. Perhaps it is worth noting that the title tradi-tionally given for the parable does not quite bring out its full implications. The parable certainly deals with a prodigal (the word means 'wasteful') son; it also deals with a waiting father who longs for the son to return in order that he may embrace him and welcome him home.

In this parable, we see a reflection of the relationship between ourselves and God. The remarkable feature of the parable is the picture of God which it gives us. The father sees the returning son long before the son notices him, and rushes out to meet him. It is clear that he has been waiting for him! Although the parable indicates that the son had come to his senses, and wanted to admit his stupidity to his father, he isn't given a chance to do this. The father embraces him before he can say a word, and makes abundantly clear the full extent of his love for the son whom he thought he would never see again. The relationship which both had thought to be lost was wonderfully restored; the celebration began!

The love of God and the death of Christ

The New Testament takes this idea of the overwhelming love of God for sinners a stage further, by specifically linking it with the death of Christ. As Paul puts it: 'God demonstrates his own love for us in this: While we were still sinners, Christ died for us' (Romans 5:8). Paul reflects upon the sort of people we might feel prepared to die for, perhaps some remarkable, outstanding person, who is clearly so good that we would have no hesitation in giving our lives in order to save theirs (Romans 5:7), but it might be difficult to think of someone like this. For Paul, this thought just brings home still further the immensity of the love of God for sinners. Even while we were still sinners, before we repented or improved ourselves, Christ died for us. Christ loved us before we were lovable. The greatest demonstration of love that human beings can manage is to give the greatest thing which they possess, life itself. There is no love greater than that of someone who gives up life itself for those whom he or she loves (John 15:13).

Examples of this are quite rare in everyday life, and are all the more memorable when we encounter them. Many date from the time of the First World War (1914–18), with its previously unimagined horrors. In many parts of northern France and Belgium, trenches were dug, in which rival armies huddled in relative safety, before being ordered to go 'over the top' into battle. The ground between the allied and German trenches was known as 'No Man's Land'. It was open and unprotected, and vulnerable to gunfire. The story is told of a soldier in the trenches of Flanders, who saw his comrade fall wounded some distance from the safety of his own lines. Rather than leave him to die, he crawled the considerable distance to where the man lay in 'No

223

Man's Land', and brought him back. As he tried to lower his friend into the trench, he himself was hit by a sniper's bullet, and mortally wounded. As he lay dying, he was told that his friend would live, and he was able to die with that knowledge. He had given his life for a friend.

Doubtless many other examples of this sort could be given. It illustrates human love forced to its absolute limits, in that the man who gives his life for his friend does not even enjoy the satisfaction of his future company. All is given, and nothing received, except perhaps an all too brief satisfaction that something worthwhile has been achieved.

The New Testament writers regarded Christ as giving his life for a definite purpose, including the powerful demonstration of the love of God for his people. But the death of Christ is about far more than that. To bring out the importance of this point, we shall explore a strongly reductionist approach to the meaning of the cross.

In the last two centuries, there has been a growing tendency in some quarters to insist that the death of Christ is nothing more than a demonstration of the love of God for us. The background to this is the rise of the movement known as the Enlightenment in the West, with its emphasis upon the total competence of human reason. Although this movement is now widely regarded as outdated and discredited, aspects of its legacy remain influential in western culture. Writers sympathetic to the Enlightenment argued that Christianity ought to be reformulated along rationalist lines.

The distinction between 'rational' and 'rationalist' needs clarification. A belief is 'rational' if it can be shown to be consistent with reason. Christian writers have always insisted that the gospel is rational, in the sense that it is consistent with the best insights of human reason. A belief is 'rationalist', however, if it is grounded only in human reason, without any appreciation of the decisive importance of divine revelation or of the severe limitations placed on unaided human thinking. At the time of the Enlightenment, unaided human reason was held to reign supreme in matters of faith. Any traditional Christian doctrines or beliefs that seemed to be out of line with reason were thus dismissed as irrational, and discarded. We have already seen how belief in the resurrection was abandoned by rationalists, on such flimsy grounds. Other beliefs were also rejected, for similar reasons. Two are of special importance in relation to an understanding of the death of Christ.

First, belief in the incarnation was abandoned on the grounds that it was 'contrary to reason'. Abandoning this central Christian belief has a major consequence. No longer is it God incarnate who dies upon the cross, but a human being. To abandon belief in the divinity of Christ is to forfeit any direct connection between God and the cross. The person who dies upon the cross is a human being, not the Son of God. The impact of this is considerable.

Secondly, it was argued that the human predicament which Christ came to remedy is simply that of ignorance concerning the nature of God. The traditional Christian view is that humanity is trapped in a situation of sin and mortality. By his death and resurrection, Christ liberates us from the bondage of sin, and opens up the possibility of eternal life. Rationalism would have none of this! Instead, the cross becomes an exercise in religious education, by which we are informed of the true nature of God.

The inadequacy of rationalist approaches

Rationalism was right in what it affirmed; however, as is so often the case, it was hopelessly wrong in what it denied. It affirmed the love of God, yet denied vital doctrines which undergirded that affirmation, including the doctrines of the incarnation and resurrection. It is certainly true that the image of Christ loving, suffering and finally dying evokes a deep response in us, and causes us to love God in return.

But there is so much more to the cross than this! These modernizing writers saw no need to involve the idea of God becoming incarnate, or the divinity of Christ, or the resurrection. For them, the death of Christ represented one human being demonstrating the love of God for humanity at large. What traditionally had been seen as one aspect of a greater whole was treated as if it was all that could be said about the meaning of the death of Christ. It is this theory which is sometimes referred to as the 'moral' or 'exemplarist' theory of the atonement, and has achieved some popularity in the more rationalist sections of the Christian church. There are, however, certain serious difficulties which must be noted in connection with it.

First, we must ask exactly how we know that the death of Christ represents a demonstration of the love of God for us. For traditional Christian belief, there is no difficulty about this whatsoever. Christ is God incarnate, and in the image of the dying Christ, we see God giving himself up for his people. One of the greats hymn of Charles Wesley (1707–88) exults in this thought:

Amazing love! how can it be
That thou, my God, shouldst die for me?

The great paradox of the immortal God giving himself up to death on behalf of the people whom he loves is nothing less than amazing, and is the theme of much reflection within the Christian tradition. To return to Wesley:

> 'Tis mystery all! th'immortal dies!
> Who can explore his strange design?
> In vain the first-born seraph tries
> To sound the depths of love divine!

By giving himself up to death, the incarnate God demonstrated the full depths of his love for us frail and mortal sinners. It is indeed the love of God with which we are dealing, in that it is none other than God himself who loved us, and gave himself for us.

Is it actually possible to get rid of the idea of Christ being God incarnate without destroying the integrity of the Christian faith, as many of those inclined towards rationalism think? Christ would then be seen as simply a man, a very special man, but a man none the less. He is therefore to be thought of as making the greatest sacrifice which any human being can make, giving his life for others. But is this the love of God? Clearly it is not. It represents the height of human love. It is, however, nothing more than human love. It shows us what the love of God might well be like, but in that, according to rationalism, Christ is not God incarnate, it is not the love of God with which we are dealing. If Christ is not God in any meaningful sense of the word, the best we can look for is information about what the love of God is (or might be) like, not a demonstration of what the love of God actually is. A messenger or delegate can tell us that, but only God himself can show us.

Why are we justified in singling out Christ as the supreme demonstration of the love of God? For the traditional Christian, the answer is evident: Christ is God incarnate, and commands our attention for that very reason. If he is not God incarnate, we must justify his uniqueness in some other way. This proves to be remarkably difficult. Outstanding human acts of love are certainly rare; during the course of human history, however, so many such acts have taken place that the best we could manage is to identify Jesus as one among many. And is there not some truth in the suggestion that the idea of the uniqueness of Christ is actually a doctrine of traditional Christianity, based upon the idea of the incarnation, which rationalism has inherited and tried to reinterpret in terms which would not establish that uniqueness in the first place? This amounts to discarding the foundations of certain doctrines, in the hope that they can survive without the support essential to their existence.

The traditional Christian ideas about Christ are retained by rationalists, yet reinterpreted in such a way that they lose their force (even if they become more credible to the sceptical mind). There are certainly those who would suggest that the idea of Jesus showing the love of God is a perfectly adequate statement of the gospel. But this version of Christianity would hardly have survived in the world into which Christianity first exploded. We are told, by its defenders, that this rationalist approach is a reinterpretation of the Christian understanding of what happened on the cross which makes sense to modern humanity. But does it really?

It is actually rather difficult to see why this idea should catch the imagination of anyone in the modern period. Humanity has always shown itself remarkably ungrateful for even the most interesting pieces of information about what God is like. On the basis of this view of the death of Christ, we are being presented with the information that God loves us. So what? After all, why should Christ's sufferings be regarded as such overwhelming demonstrations of divine love?

Unless we are involved in some terrible predicament, and unless Christ's death could be shown to be directly related to that predicament, it is difficult to see why we should be even remotely interested in, or grateful to, Jesus. Once we start talking about 'our predicament', we are moving on to rather different understandings of the significance of the death of Christ!

The 'moral' or 'exemplarist' theory of the atonement seems to presuppose that our basic problem is that of ignorance: we do not know what God is really like. We may think that God doesn't love us, but the death of Jesus on the cross educates us, by informing us that God really does love us, despite all appearances to the contrary. The theory appeals to those inclined to rationalism because it seems to eliminate ideas which they find difficult, such as the incarnation, resurrection, or human bondage to sin. But it just isn't that simple! Is it really the love of God which is revealed? A more credible interpretation is that it is a splendid example of human love – one man's love for another – which is revealed. What point did it serve? Nobody (except possibly Barabbas!) can be said to have benefited directly from the death of Jesus Christ. The idea of Jesus dying to make some sort of theological point also strains the imagination somewhat. Why did God reveal that he loved us in such a strange way? Why did it take the death of Jesus to prove this? Why couldn't God just have told us that he loved us, instead of going about conveying exactly the same information in such a complicated and ambiguous way? Ambiguous? Yes – because it is far from clear what information, if anything, is being revealed about God.

Traditional Christianity has always insisted that the cross represents, among other things, the disclosure of the full extent of God's love for sinners. Working on the basis of a theology of the incarnation (the belief that it is God who is himself present in Christ on the cross), this idea makes perfect sense. But if the theology of the incarnation is discarded, in order to make way for a simpler view of the death of Christ, what are we left with? What reasons do rationalists have for suggesting that it is the love of God which is being revealed? The death of Jesus on the cross might well demonstrate that God abandons to death those who naively trust in him (remember, rationalism discarded the resurrection as 'irrational' – there was no gospel of the risen Christ to proclaim; only the message of a dead religious teacher). It might mean that God is totally uninvolved in his world, or that the cross only reveals the terrible wrath of God directed against those who try to serve him faithfully.

These ideas are totally excluded by the traditional framework within which the death of Jesus is set, above all the doctrines of the incarnation and resurrection. To remove these doctrines is like taking away the keystone of a stone bridge; it removes its support and causes it to collapse. Why can rationalists reject the idea that the terrible death of a wonderful man like Jesus shows that God is an arbitrary tyrant, who enjoys inflicting suffering on the innocent? How can rationalists maintain the idea that the cross reveals the love of God, when they have discarded the ideas that ensure this interpretation of the cross? After all, it is not the most obvious of explanations! In the Jewish context of the first century, a cruci-fixion without a resurrection would mean simply and solely that the crucified person had died under a curse from God (Deuteronomy 21:23; Galatians 3:13). The resurrection overturns that judgment, while rationalism looks on helplessly, knowing that it is trapped within that judgment. No resurrection, no vindication of Christ, no positive meaning to the cross, and no gospel.

Traditional Christianity has, on the basis of its under-standing of the incarnation and resurrection, rightly insisted that the cross reveals the love of God. This idea has been taken over by rationalism, although it has discarded the vital theological framework which gave and guaranteed this explanation. As a result, this theory of the atonement is ultimately dependent upon a theology of the incarnation and resurrection, and logical consistency demands that this be recognized. In other words, this rationalist theory of the atonement is actually much more complicated than might at first be thought. The divinity and resurrection of Jesus Christ are the unacknowledged bulwarks of any theory which declares that the death of Christ demonstrates the love of God.

A further point we might consider is the following: God can be left out of a theory of the atonement purely as an example of love with the greatest of ease, and apparently without making much difference. As we have seen, if Jesus is not God incarnate, we are not talking about a revelation of the love of God, but a purely human love. If Jesus shows us the limits of one human being's love for another, and inspires us to imitate his example, why do we need to bring God into the theory? It works perfectly well without him. It is simply a form of moralism, providing us with information about the way in which we ought to behave, rather than with reliable information about God. Christ is treated as a moral example, showing us what we are capable of. He is an example of what every one of us could be. He is different in degree, and not in kind, from the rest of us. But why is Jesus special? We have been fortunate enough to have lots of splendid moral and religious teachers in the course of history, showing in their lives the principles which they taught.

The traditional answer to this question is perfectly straightforward: the resurrection demonstrates Jesus' identity as the Son of God, expressed in the doctrine of the incarnation. Jesus is special because of his unique relationship to God. If this view of the identity and significance of Jesus is abandoned, the special place which Christians give Jesus will have to be justified on some other grounds. But on what grounds? The excellence of his moral teaching? But Christians have tended to treat Jesus' teaching with great respect because of who they knew he was, rather than working out who he was on the basis of what he taught! Christians just don't follow Jesus as you might follow Socrates or Gandhi (people whose lives and views do indeed deserve to be respected) in the way this theory suggests. Once more, we see that this theory of the atonement is simply derivative or parasitic. In the end, it depends upon insights drawn from the framework of traditional Christianity, which rationalism discards. Whether it can actually do this is open to serious question.

Finally, it must be asked whether this theory of the atonement has a realistic view of human nature. Is fallen and sinful human nature really capable of recognizing the death of Christ as a revelation of the love of God, and responding to it? What happens if our will is so corrupted that we are incapable of making a response like this? Tennyson's famous words in his great poem *In Memoriam* seem hopelessly idealist: 'We needs must love the highest when we see it.' The more cynical observation of antiquity seems much closer to our experience: 'we see the good, and approve of it, but we go and do something worse.'

Earlier, we saw how Christians worshipped and adored Jesus as their Saviour and Lord, praying to him and praising him as if he were God himself. The view of Jesus expressed in the 'moral' or 'exemplarist' theory of the atonement doesn't fit in with this at all. It is certainly true that the death of Christ demonstrates the love of God for us. But this love of God is grounded in the idea of the one who was rich beyond all splendour, becoming poor for our sake. As the Nicene Creed puts it, 'for us and for our salvation, he came down from heaven'. We might go back to Charles Wesley's famous hymn:

> He left his father's throne above,
> So free, so infinite his grace.
> Emptied himself of all but love,
> And bled for Adam's helpless race.

The full wonder of the love of God for us can only be appreciated when we recognize what the incarnation and crucifixion really mean. Though angered and grieved by our sin, God humbles himself and stoops down to meet us where we are. The first Christians believed, as we still believe, that Jesus was the embodiment of God, God incarnate, God giving himself to us. In the incarnation, we see God giving his own self. At Calvary, God took upon himself the suffering, the pain and the agony of the world. God showed the full extent of his love by coming and suffering himself – not by sending a messenger or a substitute. It helps to know that in the seemingly sense-less and pointless suffering of Jesus, God himself is present, sharing in the tragedies of the human race. Jesus did not come to explain away, or to take away, suffering. He came to take it upon himself, to assume human suffering, and lend it dignity and meaning through his presence and sympathy. It is this which is the full-blooded meaning of the love of God, rather than the anaemic travesty of this idea to be found in the 'moral' theory of the atonement.

In contemplating the spectacle of Jesus dying on the cross, we come to see none other than God taking upon himself the agony of the world which he created and loves. It is this which is the 'love of God' in the full-blooded sense of the word. The English poet John Donne (1571–1631) expresses such thoughts like this:

Wilt thou love God, as he thee? then digest
My soul, this wholesome meditation,
How God the Spirit, by angels waited on
In heaven, doth make his temple in thy breast.
The Father having begot a Son most blessed,
And still begetting (for he ne'er begun)
Hath deigned to choose thee by adoption,
Coheir to his glory, and Sabbath's endless rest;
And as a robbed man, which by search doth find
His stol'n stuff sold, must lose or buy it again:
The Son of glory came down, and was slain,
Us whom he had made, and Satan stol'n, to unbind.
T'was much, that man was made like God before,
But, that God should be made like man, much more.

In its deepest sense, this love is that of a God who stoops down from heaven to enter into our fallen world, with

234

all its agony and pain, culminating in the grim cross of Calvary. If there is no incarnation, then there is no entering of God into our world. God remains as distant and remote as ever. But the incarnation safeguards this vital Christian insight – that God loved us so much that he was prepared to come into our sinful situation, and meet us where we are.

We could extend the parable of the prodigal son to say that God himself went into the far country, to meet us and bring us home. Earlier, we noted the story from the First World War of the soldier who went out into No Man's Land – the 'far country' – from the safety of his trench, in order to bring his beloved comrade home. He did; but it cost him his life. We left out one part, the final part, of that story. As the soldier lay dying, knowing that he had saved his friend, he whispered 'I brought him through'. The Son of God went into the far country and brought us through, brought us home, though it cost him his life. It is this astonishing love of God which lies at the heart of the gospel proclamation.

Why is this overwhelming love of God for us so important? Love gives meaning to life, in that the person loved becomes special to someone, assumes a significance which he or she otherwise might not have. There is every danger that we will feel lost and overwhelmed in the immensity of the world. What place do we have in it? Are we in any way special? Christianity makes the astonishing assertion, which it bases upon the life, death and resurrection of Jesus Christ, that God is profoundly interested in us and concerned for us, despite our apparent indifference to him. Furthermore, God is understood to give the fulness of his loving attention to each and every one, the totality of his own personal interest.

The experience of love is perhaps one of the deepest and most important that human existence knows. Take two people, one of whom cares passionately for the other, yet keeps quiet about it. Then the other finds out, perhaps by chance – and realizes that she means something special to someone else, that a new relationship is possible, that at least in the eyes of one other person she is important and precious. That moment of recognition can be devastating, and from that moment, life may be seen in a very different light. So it is with God: the realization that we mean something to God, that Christ died for us and came to bring us back from the far country to our loving and waiting Father, means that we are special in the sight of God. In the midst of an immense and frightening universe, we are given meaning and significance by the realization that the God who called the world into being, who created us, also loves us and cares for us, coming down from heaven and going to the cross to prove the full extent of that love to a disbelieving and wondering world.

Part 4

Conclusion

13

The attraction of Jesus Christ

Who is Jesus Christ? Why is he so important for Christians? And how can he transform the situations of those outside the Christian faith? These are the questions which have dominated this book. As we emphasized at the beginning, there is a very close connection between the person and the work of Jesus Christ, between who Jesus is and what he achieved for us. Although this book has focussed especially on the identity of Jesus, we have also explored some of the ways in which Christians have understood the meaning of Christ's death, and its relevance for us today.

In the late seventeenth century, the English scientist Isaac Newton discovered that a beam of white light, when passed through a glass prism, was split into a beam containing all the colours of the rainbow. The prism didn't create those colours, which had always been there in the beam of light – it just enabled them to be separated from each other and seen individually. Much the same sort of process leads to the formation of a rainbow, with raindrops acting as prisms. So it is with our reflections on Jesus Christ. Just as the prism showed up the many components of a beam of white light, so we have tried to identify and explore the many ideas and insights which are contained in the death and resurrection of Jesus Christ, and look at them individually. They haven't been invented; they have just been uncovered and isolated, in order that they may be appreciated to their full. But in the end they are all part and parcel of one and the same thing – the person of Jesus Christ, who is our Saviour.

In his celebrated work *A Study of History*, the noted historian Arnold Toynbee surveys the different types of 'saviours' who had appeared on the stage of human history. Some saviours declared that the salvation of the world lay in restoring the past glories of peoples or nations. Others insisted that the salvation of the world depends upon looking ahead to the future, to a new coming order which will remedy all the ills of the world when it arrives, and sweep the pain and sorrows of the past away. Some have been 'saviours with a sword', political and military leaders who have tried to impose their programmes of salvation by force. Others have been 'saviours of the mind', philosophers seeking to save humanity by their ideas.

Toynbee's final assessment of the achievements of such saviours is deeply pessimistic. All have failed. All have proved unable to prevent the disintegration of peoples and civilizations. None was able to deliver humanity from its final and most tragic predicament – death. All, that is, except one. As Toynbee remarks, surveying the wreckage of the human hopes of salvation, 'As we stand and gaze with our eyes fixed upon the farther shore, a single figure rises from the flood and straightway fills the whole horizon. There is the Saviour.' There is Jesus Christ, crucified for our salvation.

The attraction of Jesus Christ

There has always been a temptation to treat Christianity as a set of interesting moral or religious ideas, which can be passed on to others by teaching or argument. Yet people cannot be argued into the kingdom of God, because what has been entrusted to the church is not so much a set of ideas, as the living reality which lies behind them. It is the crucified and risen Christ who stands at the centre of the Christian faith – a person, not a set of ideas. We can be taught a set of ideas; we have to encounter and respond to Jesus Christ. It is often said that faith is 'caught, not taught'. The point which this statement makes is simply that there is far more to Christianity than a set of ideas, rules or beliefs, and that assent to these is not the same as the experience of encountering Jesus Christ. Faith is not just about accepting certain ideas to be true; it is about trusting in Jesus Christ as a personal Saviour and Lord. The cross reminds us that the central question we once were forced to ask ourselves, and which we must subsequently force others to ask, is not 'Do you believe this idea? or that idea?', but 'Who do you say Jesus Christ is?'

There is a story which is told (in a number of versions!) about the British philosopher Bertrand Russell. One day he was walking down one of Oxford's many lanes, thinking great philosophical thoughts, when he suddenly stopped, and said to himself: 'The ontological argument is right after all!' (In other words, he came to the conclusion that a certain philosophical proof for the existence of God was valid.) On another day, somewhat earlier in human history, Saul of Tarsus was walking down a different road, when he encountered the risen Christ. Russell had an idea; Saul met a person. There is all the difference in the world between these two experiences. That encounter with the risen Christ gave rise to a set of ideas. Lying behind them, however, as their source and origin was the risen Christ.

Many years ago, the evangelist L. Stanley Jones became involved in a discussion with Mahatma Gandhi about the nature and relevance of Christianity. Gandhi, who played a major role in bringing about the formation of modern India, could see Jesus Christ as nothing other than a moral teacher. Gandhi was impressed by the moral teaching of Christ, and wrote to Jones to tell him so. Exasperated, Jones penned the following lines in reply: 'you have found the principles, yet missed the person.'

The Christian experience is that the person of Jesus Christ continues to exercise a fascination over people, today as in those days when he walked by the shores of Lake Galilee. There is something about him which draws people to him – something which distinguishes him from all others who have ever lived. He alone is the 'bread of life' (John 6:48–58) who is able to meet the deep spiritual hunger and thirst of humanity. By feeding on him, a hungry and weary humanity is able to find consolation and rest.

We live in a cynical modern world, in which anyone who claims to bring good news is met with intense scepticism. Weary of promises which have not been kept and claims which have not proved to be reliable, the world has come to believe that anyone who promises joy and fulfilment has a hidden agenda of exploitation. It is suspicious of anyone who offers something precious as a gift, believing that a huge invoice will arrive by the next mailing. The world thus finds it difficult to take seriously the news of a saviour who gave his life in order that others might live. It holds back, fearing deception. And holding back, it misses the opportunity of eternal life.

This book has tried to show that this gift of eternal life is for real, and that the cost of our redemption has been borne by God himself. It has tried to reassure those who are still wondering about the love of God, where Jesus Christ fits into the great drama of redemption, and what must be done if we are to benefit from it. So important are these points that we shall explore them once more, before bringing this book to its final conclusion.

A simple approach to the cross

The impact and relevance of the cross could be summarized very simply in four familiar images or pictures, which help illustrate the meaning of the cross, and draw on ideas we have already discussed. There is much more that could be said about the cross, as we have tried to show, and it could be said a lot better and more profoundly than this – but these four points should be helpful as 'discussion starters'.

The cross as the place where we encounter God

Imagine that you are driving along a country road, perhaps at night. As you drive along, your headlights pick up a sign at the side of the road. It has a cross on it. What does it mean? It means that there is a crossroads ahead, and that means oncoming traffic. Unless you are careful, you may find yourself in collision with another vehicle. A cross here means 'a point of meeting'. And so it is with the cross of Christ. We meet God at the cross. It is through this cross that God discloses himself to us, calls to us, and meets us. Christianity is about coming to the foot of the cross, recognizing that in some strange and mysterious way, the same God who made heaven and earth makes himself available for us at this very place. In the cross and resurrection of Jesus, we recognize that he is none other than God himself, humbling himself, even to death on a cross, in order to bring us home from the far country.

The parable of the prodigal son (Luke 15:11–32) is a very moving and vivid illustration of the love of the father for his wayward son. Perhaps the thought of Jesus dying upon the cross suggests that we might change this parable slightly to bring out the full-blooded meaning of the death of Christ: the father goes after the son, into the far country, and brings him home, despite the appalling cost of this venture to himself. It is God who comes to meet us, who searches us out and finds us, to bring us home to him. In that dreadful image of the dying crucified Christ, we are presented with the sight of God, raised up high upon the cross, drawing people to himself. 'See, my servant will be raised and lifted up and highly exalted' (Isaiah 52:13). Only now do we realize the full significance of those prophetic remarks. The servant was indeed exalted and lifted up – not exalted in status, by being made a king, but by being raised up upon the cross, in order that a loveless and sinful world might see and wonder (John 3:14–15; 12:32–33).

The cross as the demonstration of our sin
Now imagine that you are back at school. You are doing some mathematics – a very simple addition, like this:

$$5 + 7 = ?$$

After much thought (remember, you're very young again!) you write the answer with a flourish.

The exasperated teacher, who had secretly hoped for much better than this, promptly scrawls a symbol by the sum to show that you are wrong. That symbol? A cross. A cross means wrong. It means not right.

In a similar way, the cross means that we are not right with God. It tells us that we are sinners, men and women who need his grace and forgiveness. We have stressed throughout this book that true forgiveness is a costly thing for God. God is loving; he is also holy and righteous. How, then, can he really forgive us sinners? He can't just say, 'Never mind, we'll pretend it never happened'. Not even we could accept that facile and superficial idea of forgiveness! In the cross of Christ, we are talking about the real forgiveness of real sins, not some sort of pretend fairy-tale stuff. God's forgiveness of sin comes about through the death of Christ on the cross – real forgiveness of real sin – in which we come face to face with both God's total condemnation of sin and his incredible and overwhelming love for us sinners. In the words of a famous hymn by the English writer Mrs Cecil F. Alexander:

> We may not know, we cannot tell,
>   What pains he had to bear;
>   But we believe it was for us,
>   He hung and suffered there.

Christ died upon the cross to take upon himself our sin. Through his suffering and death, perhaps in a way we shall never understand, God was able to forgive our sin. This astonishing fact should make us get down on our knees in wonder, rather than rush to theorize about the mechanics of the process! In the end, the most appropriate response to the cross of Christ is adoration, not theological speculation.

The gospel tells us that we are far from God, lost in a dark world, and desperately needing hope, meaning and love. The feeling of 'lostness' might make us wonder if there is, in fact, anyone who is ever going to meet us and find us. The cross of Christ tells us that, even though we are sinners, God has not forsaken us, but has taken the initiative in meeting us and finding us. Christ's suffering and death upon the cross were for us. He died to show us how far we are from God, and at the same time to open the way back to God. The cross exposes sin, and shows how its power and guilt can be broken. The cross stands at the centre of the Christian faith, revealing both the seriousness of human sin, and the purpose and power of God to deal with it.

When you think of sin as guilt, think of Christ as bearing our sin upon the cross; when you think of sin as despair, reflect upon the hope we have set before us in Christ's victory over death; when you think of sin as being far from God, rejoice in the fact that God has met us in Christ, and offered to bring us home. 'I am the way, the truth and the life' (John 14:6). We are not shown the way, and then left to make our journey unaided. Like the shepherd, God guides us along that way, travelling with us (Psalm 23 is worth reading again in this connection).

The cross, then, brings judgment. We must not, however, think of this judgment as something that is purely negative, in which God just blames us, or shows up how inadequate we are for the fun of it. Perhaps another everyday situation in which judgment is given may help bring this point out. When a doctor diagnoses an illness, he or she is passing judgment on you, telling you what is wrong with you; but telling you what is wrong in order that you may be cured. Diagnosis must never be confused with condemnation. If we are told that we are seriously ill, we condemn ourselves if we refuse to act on the basis of our knowledge of what is wrong with us on the one hand, and how that situation may be remedied on the other.

In order to be cured, we need to know what is wrong with us. It is remarkable how many people who are ill are quite unaware of the fact. They just accept their situation as normal, unaware that something is wrong, and that something can be done about it. The first step in the process of healing is identifying what the problem is. So it is with the judgment passed upon us in the cross of Christ – a judgment which identifies that something is terribly wrong with humanity, and thus opens the way to healing, transformation and renewal. The idea of Christ as the 'light of the world' (John 8:12) is especially helpful here. Light shows up things for what they really are, bringing everything to light, and making clear the dilemma with which we are faced. The cross offers a diagnosis of the human situation, as the first step towards transforming it.

In an earlier chapter, we pointed out how 'salvation' can be understood in terms of 'healing'. This allows us to take the medical analogy explored above a little further. The cross declares that we are ill. Without healing, we shall die. Yet alongside that judgment is set the news that the same gospel which diagnosed our illness is able to offer us healing. Think of the gospel as being like a medicine, like pencillin, which is able to transform our hopeless situation. Yet medicine is power-less to help a seriously ill person, unless they take it.

They need to allow its healing properties to get to work on their biological systems. So it is with the gospel. We need to connect up with Jesus Christ, through trusting in him, before he is able to transform us as he promises to do.

The cross as the demonstration of God's love

Imagine that you are writing a letter to someone very dear to you. Perhaps you are sending a Valentine card, or a very personal letter. You write it, sign it, and then indicate your affection for the person who will receive the letter by placing a series of crosses at the bottom. Crosses mean love. The cross brings home to us the full extent of God's amazing love for his people. 'God so loved the world that he gave his one and only Son' (John 3:16). 'God demonstrates his own love for us in this: While we were still sinners, Christ died for us' (Romans 5:8).

It is an astonishing thought that God actually loves us personally. It seems strange and impossible. There is simply no limit to the love of God for us. As Christ was dying upon the cross, those around him made fun of him. 'Come down from the cross', they screamed. 'Save yourself!' But he didn't. He stayed where he was, and died, showing that there was no limit to his love for us. There was simply nothing more that could be given than his own life. 'Save yourself', the crowd shouted. Yet Jesus died in order to save us instead. The words of a famous old English Christmas hymn are helpful here:

O may we keep and ponder in our mind
God's wondrous love in saving lost mankind.
Trace we the Babe, who hath retrieved our loss,
From his poor manger to his bitter cross;

248

Tread in his steps, assisted by his grace,
Till man's first heavenly state again takes place.

God, in his tender mercy, set forth on the humiliating
and costly journey to the far country, to meet his lost
children, and bring them home. Like the good shepherd,
he was prepared to lay down his life for his sheep (John
10:11).

The cross demands a decision

There is a fourth way in which we might use a cross in
everyday life. Placing a cross against a name on a ballot
paper means you are voting for them – it means that you
are making a decision. The cross of Jesus Christ also
demands a decision. God offers us love, forgiveness and
reconciliation through the cross. This offer forces us to
make a decision: will we respond to it or not? Forgiveness or reconciliation offered and not accepted does not
transform a relationship. In effect, God has given us the
immense privilege of saying 'No' to his offer of love. He
knocks on the door, gently, seeking admission (Revelation 3:20–21), but we must open the door.

A favourite sermon analogy for this during the
Middle Ages was the opening of a shutter. Suppose that
you are in a dark room, and want it lit up. The shutter
is closed, and the sunlight is beaming down upon that
shutter. The light will not enter that room and illuminate
it until you open that shutter. So it is with the forgiving
grace of God. Like the sunlight, it is always there, at our
disposal. But a decision, an action, is required if it is to
influence us or affect us. Opening that shutter to let the
light in is just like saying 'Yes' to God's offer of grace.

A famous poem by the German writer Angelus
Silesius (1624–77) has been quoted much in the present

century by theologians who wish to draw attention to the need for what they refer to as the 'personal appropriation of the gospel'. The important lines read like this:

Were Christ a thousand times to Bethlehem come,
And yet not born in you, it would spell your doom.
Golgotha's cross, it cannot save from sin,
Unless for you that cross is raised within.
I say, it helps you not that Christ is risen,
If you yourself are still in death's dark prison.

As this poem makes clear, the incarnation, crucifixion and resurrection are of little relevance to anyone unless they are received and appropriated by faith. Christ was born in Bethelehem; he must be born in us if he is to do us any good. Christ died on the cross of Calvary; unless we make that cross our own, unless we accept and receive its power by faith, it remains a distant, remote and not particularly relevant event. The great gap of space and time which separates us from the death and resurrection of Jesus Christ is bridged by faith, in order to grasp and appropriate what is on offer. Faith, to use John Calvin's famous analogy, is like an empty, open hand stretched out towards God, with nothing to offer and everything to receive. Faith is the final step in the process begun by the cross of Christ. We recognize its meaning, we realize its relevance, and finally we receive its benefits.

Conclusion

In this book, we have been concerned with exploring the various ways of understanding the full significance of Jesus Christ, and his relevance for us. There are many matters which have been discussed all too briefly, and an embarrassingly large number of questions which have not been discussed at all. It is, however, hoped that this book will stimulate its readers to begin to think further for themselves on the full relevance of Jesus Christ.

The 'message of the cross' (1 Corinthians 1:18) is the message of a God who loved his wayward children to the point where he stooped down from heaven to meet them, and suffered and died upon the cross to demonstrate the full extent of his overwhelming compassion and care for those whom he loves. God journeyed into the far country, enduring its suffering, pain and agony, to meet us and embrace us. Like a great beacon, the cross stands as a sign summoning us to discover the 'God and Father of our Lord Jesus Christ', the God of the cross, who counted us worthy of so great a sacrifice. Why should God love sinners? Why did the cross have to happen? In the end, these questions are important for theologians. The important point for all of us is that the cross did happen, and that 'the word of the cross' is that, astonishing and incredible though it may seem, God loves us and gives himself for us.

Like a beacon on a hill, the cross stands as a symbol of hope in despair, life in the midst of death, light in the darkness. 'I, when I am lifted up from the earth, will draw all men to myself' (John 12:32). Then, as now, the cross radiates with the power, love and compassion of God. It is the bread of life waiting to satisfy the hunger of men and women. In the words of the fourteenth-century writer Thomas à Kempis:

There is no salvation of soul, no hope of eternal life, except in the cross. Therefore, take up the cross, and go forward into eternal life. Christ has gone there before you, bearing his cross. He died for you upon the cross, that you may bear your cross, and die on the cross with him. For if you die with him, you will live with him; if you share his sufferings, you will share his glory.

Through the cross, God meets us in our lostness and finds us, setting us on the road which leads home – a road on which Christ has gone before us, blazing a trail we may follow, knowing that by doing so, we pass from despair to hope, and from death to eternal life.

For further reading

To keep the text of this work as simple as possible, extended scholarly discussion of the points at issue has been omitted. The following works develop the basic ideas set out in this book, and are recommended for further reading and study. Those indicated with an asterisk are especially suitable as introductions.

Baillie, D. M., *God was in Christ* (London: Faber, 1956).

Barclay, W., *Jesus as They Saw Him* (London: SCM Press, 1962).

*Bauckham, R., France, R. T., Maggay, M., Stamoolis, J. and Thiede, C. P., *Jesus 2000: A Major Investigation into History's Most Intriguing Figure* (Oxford: Lion, 1989).

Brown, R. E., *Jesus, God and Man: Modern Biblical Reflections* (Milwaukee: Bruce, 1967).

Bruce, F. F., *The Gospel of John* (Grand Rapids: Eerdmans, 1983).

—, 'Our God and Saviour: A Recurring Biblical Pattern', in S. G. F. Brandon (ed.), *The Saviour God* (New York: Barnes & Noble, 1963), pp. 51–66.

Caird, G. B., *The Language and Imagery of the Bible* (Philadelphia: Westminster, 1980).

Carson, D. A., *The Gospel According to John* (Grand Rapids: Eerdmans, 1991).

Cousar, C. B., *A Theology of the Cross: The Death of*

Jesus in the Pauline Letters (Minneapolis: Fortress Press, 1990).

Cullmann, O., *The Christology of the New Testament* (Philadelphia: Westminster Press, 1959).

Davis, S. T., *Risen Indeed: Making Sense of the Resurrection* (Grand Rapids: Eerdmans, 1993).

Dawe, D. G., *Jesus: The Death and Resurrection of God* (Atlanta, GA: John Knox, 1987).

*Drane, J., *Jesus and the Four Gospels* (Oxford: Lion, 1984).

Dunn, J. D. G., *Christology in the Making* (London: SCM Press, 1980).

—, *The Evidence for Jesus* (London: SCM Press, 1986).

Erickson, M. J., *The Word Became Flesh* (Grand Rapids: Baker, 1991).

France, R. T., *Jesus and the Old Testament* (Downers Grove, Ill: InterVarsity Press, 1971).

*—, *The Evidence for Jesus* (London: Hodder & Stoughton, and Downers Grove, Ill: InterVarsity Press, 1987).

Grillmeier, A., *Christ in Christian Tradition* (2nd edn) (London: Mowbrays, 1976).

*Green, M., *Who is this Jesus?* (London: Hodder & Stoughton, 1990).

Gunton, C. E., *Yesterday and Today: A Study of Continuities in Christology* (London: Darton, Longman and Todd, and Grand Rapids: Eerdmans, 1983).

Harris, M. J., *From Grave to Glory: Resurrection in the New Testament* (Grand Rapids: Zondervan, 1990).

—, *Jesus as God: The New Testament Use of Theos in Reference to Jesus*. (Grand Rapids: Baker, 1992).

Hooker, M. D., 'Interchange in Christ', *Journal of Theological Studies* 22 (1971), pp. 349–61.

Käsemann, E., 'The Saving Significance of the Death of

Jesus in Paul', in *Perspectives on Paul* (Philadelphia: Fortress Press, 1971), pp. 32–59.

Lapide, P., *The Resurrection of Jesus* (Philadelphia: Fortress Press, 1987).

Linnemann, E., *Historical Criticism of the Bible: Methodology or Ideology? Reflections of a Bultmannian turned Evangelical* (Grand Rapids: Baker, 1990).

Loader, W. R. G., *The Christology of the Fourth Gospel* (New York/Berne: Lang, 1989).

*McGrath, A. E., *Making Sense of the Cross* (Leicester: Inter-Varsity Press, 1992). North American edition published as *What was God Doing on the Cross?* (Grand Rapids: Zondervan, 1993).

—, *The Making of Modern German Christology 1750–1990* (2nd edn) (Leicester: Inter-Varsity Press and Grand Rapids: Zondervan, 1993).

*—, *Christian Theology: An Introduction* (Oxford: Blackwell, 1994), pp. 270–308; 337–368.

Macquarrie, J., *Jesus Christ in Modern Thought* (London: SCM Press, 1990).

Martin, R. P., *Carmen Christi: Philippians 2:5–11 in Recent Interpretation and in the Setting of Early Christian Worship* (Cambridge: Cambridge University Press, 1967).

Marshall, I. H., *The Origins of New Testament Christology* (Downers Grove, Ill: InterVarsity Press, 1976).

Mascall, E., *Theology and the Gospel of Christ* (London: SPCK, 1977).

Miller, E. L., *Salvation History in the Prologue of John* (Leiden: Brill, 1989).

Morris, L., *The Apostolic Preaching of the Cross* (3rd edn) (Leicester: Inter-Varsity Press, 1975).

— *Jesus is the Christ* (Grand Rapids: Eerdmans, 1989).

Moule, C. F. D., *The Origin of Christology* (Cambridge:

Cambridge University Press, 1977).

O'Collins, G., *Jesus Risen* (London: Darton, Longman and Todd, 1987).

Pannenberg, W., *Jesus – God and Man* (London: SCM Press, and Westminster: Philadeplhia, 1968).

Pollard, T. E., *Johannine Christology and the Early Church* (Cambridge: Cambridge University Press, 1970).

Sanders, J. T., *The New Testament Christological Hymns* (Cambridge: Cambridge University Press, 1971).

Sayers, D. L., *Creed or Chaos and Other Essays in Popular Theology* (London: Methuen, 1947).

Sellers, R. V., *Two Ancient Christologies: A Study in the Christological Thought of the Schools of Alexandria and Antioch* (London: SPCK, 1954).

*Stott, J. R. W., *The Cross of Christ* (Leicester: Inter-Varsity Press, 1986).

Theissen, G., *The Shadow of the Galilean* (London: SCM Press, 1987).

Thiede, C. P., *Jesus – Life or Legend* (Oxford: Lion, 1990).

Toynbee, A. J., *A Study of History* (2nd edn) (London: Oxford University Press, 1939).

Wells, D. F., *The Person of Christ: A Biblical and Historical Analysis of the Incarnation* (Westchester, Ill.: Crossway, 1984).

Wright, N. T., *Who was Jesus?* (London: SPCK and Grand Rapids: Eerdmans, 1992).